Who doesn't love sandwi... wouldn't love this mouthwa... of 85+ recipes for sandwic... of all kinds?

CHANCES ARE you have a favorite sandwich, or maybe two, or six, or ten! We can all agree that sandwiches are fun; they're delicious, they're comforting, and they're as easy to make as it comes. In short, sandwiches are a damn good thing.

In *The Book of Sandwiches*, you'll find sandwich recipes for every day of the week and every week of the year. Sandwiches for comfort food cravings, for quick meals to grab and go, even for high-impact (low-key) ways to impress your friends. (Make someone a great sandwich and you've got a friend for life!) Inside are sandwiches for late nights when the hunger hits, and for the next morning when your energy is low . . . Try the very best new versions of well-known sandwiches, plus tons of truly inventive ideas for sandwiches you've never thought of before. Included are recipes for:

The Classics

Enjoy fresh takes on the quintessential sandwiches we all love, like timeless grilled cheeses, a simply sensational toasted tomato sandwich, and the beloved BLT.

Breakfast

What better way to start your day than with a sandwich? Here are options galore—egg, cheese, avocado, bacon, sausage, or even homemade granola (granola in a sandwich?! Just you wait!).

Chic

Dial it up a notch with stylish (dare we say fancy?) sandwiches like The Wild Duck, the Soft-Shell Crab, or our beautiful Cover Model, starring fried chicken.

Open

Ditch the tops for these delicious and beautiful rule-bending recipes.

Burgers

If a beef, turkey, chicken, fish, or portobello mushroom burger isn't a sandwich, then what is?

Hot Hot Mess

Indulge in sandwiches like The Meatball, the Ragù for You, and even the It's a Hawaiian Pizza Sandwich!—just remember the napkins!

Sweet

Satisfy that sweet tooth with ice cream sandwiches, cookie sandwiches, and whoopie pies aplenty!

PAGE AFTER PAGE, this book's mouthwatering photography unveils the potential of everyone's favorite food, with recipes you'll be running into the kitchen to try. This really is *the* book of sandwiches.

" **Make someone a great sandwich, and you've got a friend for life.** "

The Book of Sandwiches

DELICIOUS TO THE LAST BITE:
RECIPES FOR EVERY SANDWICH LOVER

JASON SKROBAR

PHOTOGRAPHY BY
SÉBASTIEN DUBOIS-DIDCOCK

appetite
by RANDOM HOUSE

Appetite by Random House® and colophon are
registered trademarks of Penguin Random
House LLC.

Library and Archives Canada Cataloguing in
Publication is available upon request.
ISBN: 978-0-525-61252-0
eBook ISBN: 978-0-525-61253-7

Photography by Sébastien Dubois-Didcock
Food styling by Jason Skrobar
Illustrations by Joel Malkin
Cover and book design by Jennifer Griffiths
Printed in China

Published in Canada by Appetite by Random
House®, a division of Penguin Random House
Canada Limited

www.penguinrandomhouse.ca

10 9 8 7 6 5 4 3 2

appetite   Penguin
by RANDOM HOUSE   Random House
                  Canada

For Mom,
my forever inspiration in the kitchen

And for Dad,
my constant reminder of why I love to cook

And for my dear Carm,
for the introduction to the world of cookbooks

CONTENTS

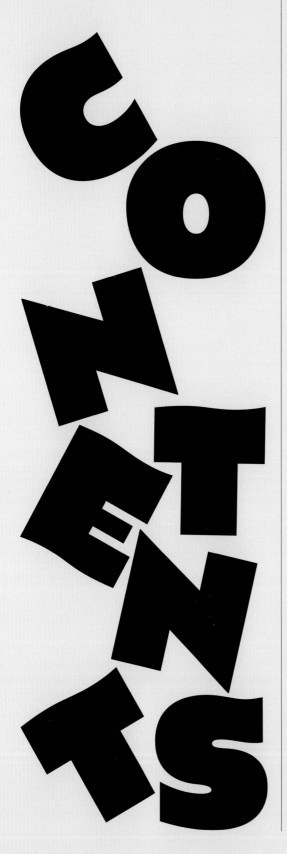

Hello, Sandwich Lovers

I remember sitting at our kitchen table when I was 6 or 7 while my mom made us her version of grilled cheese sandwiches for me and my brothers, Greg, Paul, and Ryan. She used fresh-baked pita from the market, luxurious European butter (my dad immigrated to Canada from Slovenia and loved it), and cheese from the cheesemonger (no prepackaged cheese singles in her kitchen!). It was simple, sure, but watching her make those sandwiches and then eating one—the crunch of the toasty, buttery pita, the melty and oozy cheese, and (some may wholeheartedly disagree with this) the sweetness of lots and lots of ketchup (hey, I was a kid after all!)—was pure joy. She often made us what we called grilled pitas, and as I grew up, I in turn made them often as well. Experimenting a bit here and there, they may not all have been hits, but I think my mom's grilled cheese pita is where my love of a good sandwich started.

Food can sometimes be a bit polarizing: Do you like cilantro? (Does it taste like soap to you, or is it a refreshing, citrusy punch of flavor?) What about anchovies? (Love their salty, briny qualities, or loathe them because you were taught they don't belong on pizza and have never given them another try?)* Wherever you stand on these things, and many others like them, it seems the one food people can agree on is the sandwich— whether it's a PB&J, a grilled cheese, a meatball sub, or a freaking burger.** People agree that the sandwich is a damn good thing. A perfect thing, indeed. Think about it. What's the best thing you can eat for breakfast? A sandwich. What do you eat for lunch? A sandwich. What do you eat late at night? A sandwich. What do you eat when you are hungover? A sandwich. Sandwiches are comforting. Sandwiches are fun. And sandwiches have the ability to bring people together. Make someone a great sandwich, and you've got a friend for life. I kid, but you get the point.

People everywhere eat sandwiches every single day. Canadians alone eat more than 3.6 billion sandwiches each year; 11.5 billion are consumed annually in the UK; and Americans—by far the most significant consumers of sandwiches in the world—eat 45 billion of them every 365 days! That's a *lot* of sandwiches. And we haven't even touched on the rest of Europe, or Australia, Asia, Africa, or South and Central America, where sandwiches play a massive part in the culinary lives of so many people who live there.

I like to think outside the box when I make sandwiches, and I hope this book will help you do the same. I remember visiting friends Morgain and Gary a few years back when I was in the UK. We went out to the pub and the kitchen was closed, so all we had to eat were a few bags of crisps (or chips, as we call them here in North America). Upon returning home, I took it upon myself to make my hosts the best sandwich I possibly could to satisfy our now all-consuming hunger. (Thankfully, their fridge had a pretty impressive amount of ingredients to choose from, but that's beside the point.) Wondering what I made? It made it into this book: The Wild Duck (page 98). It was a beautiful concoction of different ingredients and my friends still say it's the best sandwich they've ever had, and hopefully, when you make that sandwich, you will agree.

Just like with anything you do often enough, monotony in sandwich making can be a real thing, so I'm excited for you to come on this ride with me and experiment a bit. Flipping through this book and seeing a recipe for a za'atar egg salad sandwich with fresh herb salad (page 31) (there's that cilantro!) or a lobster roll with anchovy mayo (page 109) (there's that anchovy!) will hopefully inspire you to step up your sandwich game a little bit—and open your eyes to the idea that a sandwich can be anything you want it to be. Let's be honest; we're not curing cancer here, so this book is really about having fun, enjoying some great recipes, and learning a few new things along the way.

I make my grilled cheeses a bit differently now (as you'll find out in the recipes in this book), but every once in a while, I'll make one just like my mom did—yes, ketchup is still involved, but now mixed with some hot sauce—and it takes me right back to where my love of sandwiches began. So thanks, Mom!

Happy sandwich making, friends, and let's meet up at the end and exchange notes.

Me, enjoying mom's homemade yogurt, age 4

Seriously, folks, give the damn anchovy a chance! Your sandwich (and pizza, salad dressing, or roasted vegetables) will love you for it!

Is a burger a sandwich? Don't worry, there's a whole chapter dedicated to that question.

" I think my mom's grilled cheese pita is where my love of a good sandwich started. "

A Sandwich Story

efore you start reading this section, I suggest you make your way to the kitchen, take a peek inside your fridge, assemble the best sandwich possible, walk back to your comfy reading chair (or lie on your bed, as I would do), and appreciate your sensational creation as you learn about the history of the very thing you are feasting on. Trust me, it will make for a much more enjoyable read.

Let's get one thing out of the way: the *Oxford English Dictionary* describes the sandwich as "Two slices of bread enclosing a filling (meat, cheese, fish, etc.)." It is an invention attributed to the 4th Earl of Sandwich (1718–92), who spent long periods at the gaming table and carried a portable meal of "beef sandwiched with bread." But *attributed* is the important word here. While the Earl of Sandwich's name may live on in the history books as the person the sandwich is named after, he by no means invented it. So if you thought that's where the story of the sandwich began, fellow sandwich lovers, I have some news for you! Are you hungry for a bit of sandwich schooling?* It's time to take a deep dive into the complex history of our beloved sandwich.

The idea of putting something between or on top of bread has been around for thousands of years. This means the natural history of the sandwich has many different beginnings, spreading across the globe and varying times throughout history. It is impossible to say precisely when and where the idea for what we know as a sandwich was first thought up. Let's look at a few historical points in time where it played a crucial role in what people ate. To do that, we need to start with bread. Where and when was bread first made? Who were the first bakers on the planet? Did the creation of bread give birth to an ancient archetype of what we now know to be the sandwich? As I said, it's a deep dive, so you might want to consider a second sandwich!

1 Our first stop is in Jordan's north-eastern Black Desert. Recent archaeological digs found evidence of charred crumbs from flatbreads baked some 14,500 years ago by the hunter-gatherers of the Natufian culture. The flatbread, made from wild cereal (most likely einkorn and barley) and tubers ground into flour, was baked in firepits. This is the earliest concrete confirmation of bread making ever recorded. While there is no evidence that these hunter-gatherers used these flatbreads as vehicles for then consuming the snakes, lizards, and gazelles they hunted, one would think (and hope!) that at least a few of them may have stumbled onto the idea. (And stumble they may have! Scientists also credit the Natufian culture as one of the first to produce alcoholic beverages, mostly beer. What a legacy—bread and beer for the win!) So we now know that flatbreads were first produced within the Fertile Crescent (which stretches from the Mediterranean Sea to the Persian Gulf). We also know that they then began to spread to other regions within that part of the world: northern Africa, the Arabian peninsula, southern Europe, the Indian subcontinent (which includes modern-day Bangladesh, Bhutan, India, Maldives, Nepal, Pakistan, and Sri Lanka), and central Asia. As flatbreads and bread making started making their way around the world, naturally, sandwiches began to emerge.

2 Our next stop is China and the province of Shaanxi, in the northern part of the country, during the Qin dynasty (221–206 BCE), where the roujiamo was born. It is loosely translated to "meat in a bun," and is sometimes referred to as a Chinese burger. The bread component of this ancient sandwich is called the baijimo and is a wheat flour flatbread bun. As with most sandwich origin stories, especially ones this old, it is hard to say for sure of exact dates and specifics, but we know it was first baked sometime during the Qin dynasty in or on the sides of clay ovens. The meat portion is believed to be even older than the flatbread, originating during the Zhou dynasty (1045 BCE–256 BCE). It's traditionally made of chopped pork belly that has been simmered in a rich broth studded with spices such as ginger, star anise and chilies. What we do know for sure is that the roujiamo is delicious, messy and still kicking it all these years later.

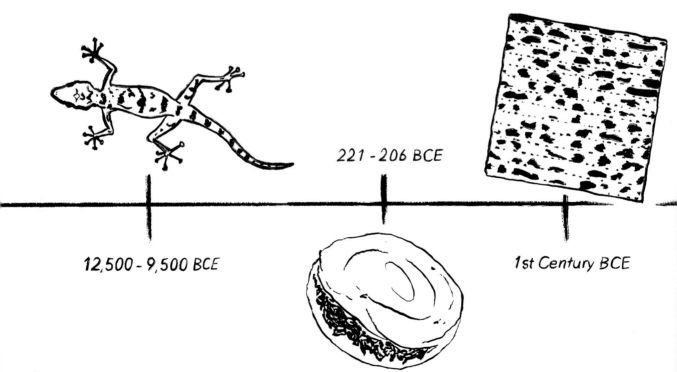

221 - 206 BCE

12,500 - 9,500 BCE

1st Century BCE

3 Next on our trip through sandwich history, we head to the 1st century BCE. Hillel the Elder, a rabbi and scholar, began the tradition of taking bitter herbs such as horseradish, bitter lettuce or sumac, and placing them between two pieces of matzo during the Passover seder. The matzo Hillel used was soft and pliable, not thin and crisp like what you commonly see today. Nowadays, the Hillel sandwich served during Passover is most likely also made with haroset, a condiment comprised of sweet fruits and nuts.

4 On to ancient Rome, sometime in 5th century CE, where we find copies of the famous Roman cookbook *Apicius*. The exact author or authors are unknown, but there are a few theories about where the recipes found in the book might have come from. Some suggest that many of them can be attributed to Marcus Gavius Apicius—a wealthy, well-known Roman gourmand who lived in the 1st century—and that the rest may have been authored by a collective of cooks who lived in and around Rome, also during the 1st century. Wealthy Romans did not cook, though, their enslaved people did, and so many believe *Apicius* was intended not for the rich but for their enslaved to cook from. For that reason, and the fact that the recipes were written in "vulgar" or "blue-collar" Latin (and not classical Latin like the upper class would write), the recipes in *Apicius* were probably authored by the enslaved people who cooked for Marcus Gavius rather than himself. The book was broken down into chapters, much like how modern cookbooks are today, and inside one of them was what I'd consider a burger recipe! Titled "Isicia Omentata," it was made of minced meat, pine nuts, fish sauce, pepper, juniper berries, and herbs and wrapped in caul fat. It was served with bread, so we could easily assume that some of the Romans eating this dish would have made a burger out of it.

5 We head next to the beginning of the European Middle Ages, where something called trenchers had begun being used. Trenchers were round, thick, stale slices of bread that folks would use as plates, placing their meat, vegetables, and sauce—or whatever their meal was—directly onto the bread. Once the meal was finished, the trenchers would then be distributed to the servants or the poor. The sauce- and oil-soaked bread made for quite the tasty treat; think about when you use the last bit of bread to

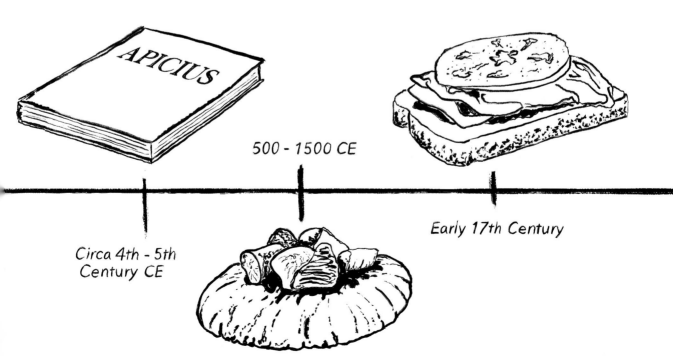

APICIUS

500 - 1500 CE

Circa 4th - 5th Century CE

Early 17th Century

mop up the last bit of sauce on your plate when finishing a meal! This practice could technically be the beginning of the open-faced sandwich, which takes us to our next stop.

6 Open-faced sandwiches have roots in many European countries: France, the UK, Poland, my homeland of Slovenia, and countless others. But none can claim the title of queen of the open-faced sandwich quite like the Scandinavian countries of Denmark, Norway, and Sweden and their smørrebrød. Smørrebrød, meaning "buttered bread," started to pop up in the early 17th century, usually consisting of rye bread with various toppings like meat, fish, cheese, condiments, herbs, and garnishes. Smørrebrød, like so many dishes in history, started as something that farmers would eat for lunch and has evolved to become a fancy dish served worldwide.

7 And here's where we meet the aforementioned earl in late-17th-century England. While yes, it is true that what we now call a sandwich is named after John Montagu, the 4th Earl of Sandwich, it should be clear by now that he was by no means the first to think of putting something between two slices of bread, picking it up, and eating it. It just never had an official name until the term *sandwich* was coined, after Montagu's insistence on having his dinner served between two slices of bread while at the gambling table. Fellow gamblers started ordering "what Sandwich is having," and thus the term stuck, giving a name to something that had never really needed one before. (But I'm sure we're all glad it has one now.)

8 We now travel to America and the early 1800s, when sandwiches started popping up in cookbooks, which were almost exclusively written by women. The sandwiches in these cookbooks were not fancy like they can be now. In fact, the first recipe for a sandwich in an American cookbook was from author Eliza Leslie in her book *Miss Leslie's Complete Cookery: Directions for Cookery, in its Various Branches,* first published in 1837. This was the most popular cookbook in America in the 19th century, and in it she introduced Americans to the ham sandwich.

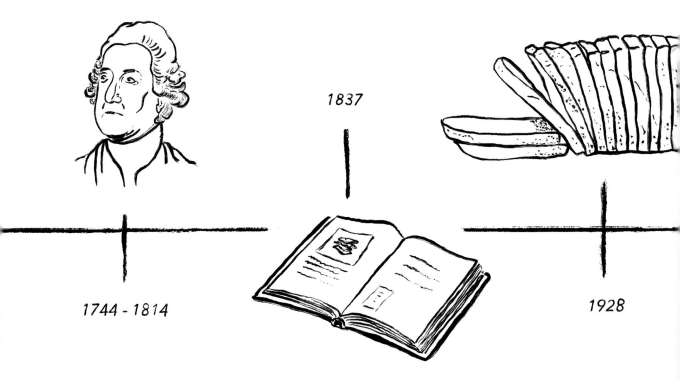

1837

1744 - 1814

1928

But the sandwich didn't really take off in America until after 1928, when Otto Frederick Rohwedder came up with what would become one of the most famous inventions of the 20th century (that might be a bit of an exaggeration, but hey, this is a sandwich cookbook after all!). What did he invent, you might be wondering? Only the greatest thing since sliced bread—Rohwedder invented the machine that literally slices bread. It took him a few tries to get it right, and by the sounds of things bakeries were not too quick to embrace the new technology, but once it took off, sliced bread became readily available and Americans started to truly fall in love with the sandwich.

 Now to our last stop, back to the UK, to the 1980s and British department store Marks & Spencer. You see, for years sandwiches were only things you would make at home, mostly from boring leftovers, and never truly inspired meals. And if you wanted them for your office or work lunch, you would wrap them up and take them with you. That all changed in 1980, when Marks & Spencer had the idea of modernizing the lunch experience and started to sell prepackaged sandwiches in some of its stores. The sandwiches they sold were not flashy (think salmon, cucumber, or egg salad), but while lunch counters had existed for some time selling hot sandwiches drenched in gravy, M&S was the first to package sandwiches and sell them to go. And they were a hit right out of the gate. Stores were selling out quickly every day, and soon this little sandwich experiment became ubiquitous, with every department store and grocery store in the UK following suit. It wasn't long before this trend traveled across the pond, and now you'll find prepackaged sandwiches everywhere in North America too, from gas stations to upscale markets.

So there you have it. By no means is this a complete list, just a few moments in the sandwich's evolution over time. A short history that led us to today's global sandwich industry that's worth billions of dollars. What to say about the future of the sandwich industry? Who knows. But I do know that if this book inspires you to make a sandwich you may otherwise not have thought of, I've played my small part in the sandwich game (and so have you).

I hope you've enjoyed reading a bit about where, when, and how the sandwich landed at the top of the culinary world. Now, let's get cooking!

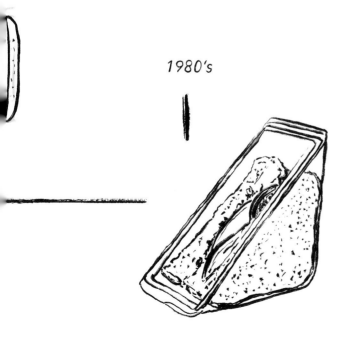

1980's

 Speaking of hungry, how's that sandwich you just made? Research indicates that the average lunchtime sandwich takes about 3–3½ minutes to eat, so you're probably halfway done. Perhaps a few drips of mayo or Dijon managed to find their way onto the book; a crumb or two as well? No matter. If used correctly, this book should be full of smears and smudges by the time you finish making every sandwich, or even if you make only some of them. Now back to our regularly scheduled sandwich story.

Building Your Perfect Sandwich

Is there such a thing as a perfect sandwich? As the famous lovestruck sign in *Love Actually* says, "To me, you are perfect." Meaning, yes, there is such a thing as perfection, but your version of a perfect sandwich might not be the same as mine. So what follows is a checklist that will help you navigate the world of sandwich making and create that perfect sandwich for you. Not every element is necessary and there are no rules here really, so feel free to go rogue at any time.

BREAD Could this be the most essential part of the sandwich? Perhaps, perhaps not. But at least we can all agree that without the bread, there would be no sandwich. I have a straightforward yet easy-to-follow rule when deciding on what bread to pair with what fillings: crunchy inside, soft outside; soft inside, crunchy outside. The reason for this is simple: you don't want the bread to compete with the filling and vice versa. Let me give you an example. Our most beautiful cover model, the fried chicken sandwich (page 95), is crunchy on the inside (very, very crunchy, in fact!), so we pair it with soft bread, and brioche is the perfect partner. Another example is the pulled lamb sandwich (page 103): soft pulled lamb paired with a nice and crunchy toasted baguette. Perfect. Of course, like with most rules, there are exceptions. A case in point is the peanut butter and jam sandwich (page 50). In this book we pair it with plain old soft white sandwich bread. So, soft on the inside *and* soft on the outside. It just works. But feel free to toast the bread if you need to stick to the rules!

Speaking of toasting, many of the breads and buns in this book are toasted. I like—no, I *love*—a toasted bun or slice of bread. Not only does it add a bit of extra texture to a sandwich, but when a sauce is smeared onto warm toasted bread, some will melt into the toast, almost becoming one with the bread, and it's truly magical. Feel free to use a toaster to toast your bread, but I prefer a skillet and some extra-virgin olive oil. To toast, I place a large skillet over medium-high heat and add a bit of oil. Let the skillet and the oil heat up, then add the bread. I toast each side (or just the cut side of a bun or baguette) until the edges are crisp and golden brown and the inside has taken on some color. Be sure to move the bread or bun around and add a touch more oil if the pan seems dry. Perfect.

The following is a list of some of the breads that appear in this book and a brief description of each:

BAGUETTE: A bread of French origin, the baguette, made of only four ingredients (flour, water, salt, and yeast), has become so iconic that it has been given world heritage status by the United Nations. Dating back to the 19th century, baguettes are synonymous with the French and pop up quite often in this book. (Funny story: I shot part of this book in Paris and did not pick any sandwiches to shoot that called for baguette. Epic fail.)

BRIOCHE: Another bread of French origin, dating back to the 1400s. Soft and light, with a slight sweetness. Works well with savory and sweet sandwiches. Along with sourdough, it's the most used bread in this book.

CIABATTA: A bread of Italian origin, although a relatively new kid on the block, having been invented in 1982 in Veneto, Italy. The baker Arnaldo Cavallari is credited with creating it as an alternative to the French baguette. The story goes that bakeries in Italy were worried about the number of baguettes imported by Italy to make sandwiches. They wanted to create an Italian version of the baguette, and the ciabatta was born. Crispy on the outside and chewy on the inside, it makes for the perfect sandwich bread.

FOCACCIA: Another bread of Italian origin, dating back to the 14th century. A flatbread with a soft and airy inside and a deliciously crusty outside (if eaten straight out of the oven). Made with rich olive oil and usually paired with herbs, it can also be made with sweet ingredients. There is a delicious recipe for focaccia in this book (page 81) and it's been paired with several sandwiches.

KAISER ROLL: Originating from Austria in the mid-1700s, this roll has four or five distinct folds in the dough that make an almost flower-like pattern. Crusty on the outside and usually chewy and soft on the inside.

MULTIGRAIN: Mixed-grain loaves of bread have been baked for centuries and can encompass various grains. Most, if not all, bakeries these days will carry some multigrain bread. Use your favorite whenever you see a multigrain pop up in a recipe.

PUMPERNICKEL: A type of rye bread, pumpernickel originates from Germany. The traditional German-produced pumpernickel is not what you might think of when you think of this bread. The centuries-old German version is made with only 100% whole-grain rye and baked in tins with covers, resulting in a loaf of bread with no crust. The traditional pumpernickel is baked at low temperatures for a very long time, ensuring its iconic dark brown color and deep and slightly sweet molasses flavor. North American and some European bakeries add wheat flour to the dough and bake it at much higher temperatures and without its unique tins; therefore, the bread takes on completely different characteristics—lighter and not so dense. This makes for two very different types of pumpernickel. The traditional type is available at most grocery stores but is usually stocked near the deli instead of the bakery. Use the non-traditional version anytime you see pumpernickel in this book.

RYE: It's almost impossible to talk about rye bread in only a few sentences, as there are many variations and types. Most European countries have their own versions, but they are usually relatively dense and tend to be dark, with a strong and sometimes slightly sour flavor. I encourage you to use your favorite rye when you see that particular bread pop up in a recipe.

SOURDOUGH: At its core, a slow-fermented bread that does not use commercial yeast to make it rise. Its tangy and slightly sharp flavor combined with a chewy inside and crispy crust make this bread a powerhouse, and it's used quite often in this book.

FILLINGS

We established that without bread, there is no sandwich, but without the filling, there also is no sandwich. So I guess these two are neck and neck in importance to the sandwich. Sandwich fillings can be anything, and they act as the anchor that defines the type of sandwich you make. A tomato sandwich, a hamburger, a grilled cheese, a Reuben, a frittata sandwich . . . I could go on, but you get it. The filling dictates the sandwich you're making. If you've got the bread, and you've got the fillings, you're almost there.

SAUCE

Ah, sauce! Lovely, lovely sauce. If you had a peek inside my fridge, you might be shocked by the number of sauces I have. I love sauce. Like, a lot! No good sandwich is without sauce. And every sandwich in this book has some type: pesto, hot sauce, BBQ sauce, mustard, mayo, mayo, mayo (there's *lots* of mayo in this book), crème fraîche, tartar sauce, maple syrup, hot honey, dressings, jams—yes, for the purpose of this book, I consider jam a sauce (do not come for me!). In fact, there is a chapter at the end of the book dedicated to the sauces I use the most. How do you decide which sauce works with the sandwich you're about to make? It's not scientific but really about deciding what complementary flavors and textures will work with the fillings you have decided upon. Start experimenting with flavor combinations and have fun pairing different sauces with different fillings.

ADD-ONS

These little finishing touches within the sandwich add to its bulk and complement the fillings. They're the background players—think tomatoes (unless it is My Perfect Sandwich (page 26), in which case the tomato is the star!), lettuce, cheese, pickles, olives, caramelized onions, bacon—but they must be well cast or they can throw the whole production out of whack. Be a good casting director and choose your add-ons wisely, or you might end up pissing off the lead actors and throwing the whole performance into turmoil.

GARNISHES

A garnish is the last hurrah before the sandwich makes its way to the table (though, in my case, it might not make it that far!). It's that last little thing that finishes the sandwich, be it a pickle or an olive on a skewer, a scattering of chopped herbs, or a sprinkling of flaky salt; sometimes it's the little things that make a big difference.

"There are no rules here really, so feel free to go rogue at any time."

The Steak Sandwich in This Book, page 54

Some Notes on Ingredients

BUTTER: In this book I use only unsalted butter, as I like to control the amount of salt in my cooking and baking. To get the most life out of your butter, keep it wrapped and stored in the fridge. Stored properly, butter will last up to 3 months. That said, I do keep a bit on my kitchen counter so I always have softened butter on hand for that late-night toast craving!

CHEESE: When buying cheese, always buy whole bricks, never pre-grated. Pre-grated cheese often contains preservatives to keep the cheese fresh.

CITRUS: One of the things you will almost always see on my kitchen counter is a bowl of citrus. I use citrus a lot, whether it's a squeeze of lemon in dressings, a zest of orange in baking or a whack-load of lime juice in a margarita, I always have them on hand. Lots of citruses are used in this book; lemons, limes, grapefruit, and oranges all make an appearance. Store your citrus at room temperature for the first 5 days after purchase and then in the crisper of your fridge for a few weeks.

EGGS: Picking the right eggs to buy can be a bit intimidating. There are free-range, cage-free, pasture-raised, brown, white, large, jumbo, organic, and farm-fresh among the countless other descriptions eggs now have. Who's to know which are the best eggs to buy? I will spare you the gritty details as to why, but for me, farm-fresh eggs are the best if you can get your hands on them; otherwise, always stick with organic. When it comes to size, I use large eggs in my recipes. And if you're wondering what the difference is between white and brown eggs, well, it's simply the color of the hen's feathers and nothing more.

FRESH FRUITS & VEGETABLES: As with fresh herbs (below), lots of fresh fruit and veg pop up in this book but you won't necessarily use it all when making the sandwiches. To extend the life of your fruits and vegetables, always wash them thoroughly when you get them home from the grocery store (except for berries, which should only be washed when you're about to use them). Storing fruits and vegetables properly will extend their life by a few days to a few weeks, depending on the variety. For veg, potatoes, sweet potatoes, garlic, onions (apart from green onions), tomatoes and squash should all be stored out of the refrigerator until they have been peeled and cut, at which point they should be wrapped and stored in the fridge. All the other veg that appear in this book should be stored in the fridge until ready for use. For fruit, apricots, nectarines, peaches, plums, avocados, and bananas should all be left out of the fridge to continue to ripen. Berries, apples, figs, grapes, and cherries will last longer if stored in the fridge.

FRESH HERBS: Herbs can be divided into two categories, delicate and hard. Delicate herbs have tender stems, like parsley, chives, cilantro, and tarragon. Hard herbs have woody stems, like rosemary, thyme, oregano, sage, and bay. Fresh herbs play a big part in this book and so you'll inevitably have leftover herbs on hand after making some of the recipes. Wash fresh herbs well, dry them thoroughly, and store them wrapped in a damp cloth or paper towel in a reusable bag in the fridge. The exception to this rule is basil, which you should store with its stems in a glass of water and cover with a reusable bag, at room temperature and never in the fridge.

HOT SAUCE: As I'm sure you are aware, thousands of hot sauces are available on the market. Unless otherwise noted, I tend to stick to vinegar-based hot sauces in this book, like a Louisiana hot sauce. It has a perfect balance of heat and flavor and does well when mixed into other sauces. But by all means, use your favorite. I know most people are pretty picky when it comes to hot sauce.

MAYONNAISE: A hero in the condiment world (and in my kitchen), there's not much to say here other than that mayonnaise is used a lot in this book, so find your favorite brand and stock up (or turn to the recipes on pages 238 and 239)! If you're looking for something new, I highly recommend trying the Japanese brand Kewpie. It's rich and beautifully tangy and I always have a bottle of it in my fridge.

MUSTARD: Grainy, Dijon, or yellow, they're all here. Stock up or make your own (there is a recipe for grainy mustard on page 242), because mustard, just like mayonnaise, is front and center in this book. Fun fact: Canada is one of the world's leading producer of mustard seeds.

OILS: Extra-virgin olive oil is used a lot in this book, as is avocado oil. Contrary to popular belief, both are well suited for frying, which there is a lot of in this book. You can also reuse both olive and avocado oil after frying. Let the oil come to room temperature, strain out any fried bits, and store it in a cool, dark place. You can reuse the oil up to five times. When buying extra-virgin olive oil, always make sure to purchase it in a dark-colored bottle, never clear, as olive oil likes to rest in the shade and not in full sunlight. Neutral oils such as grapeseed or sunflower also come into play in the book, particularly when deep frying, as those recipes call for a significant amount of oil and I don't want you to break the bank over a fried chicken sandwich.

PEPPER: Always use freshly cracked black pepper, never the lifeless pre-ground stuff. Invest in a good quality pepper mill and you'll never look back.

SALT: In cooking and baking, I always use kosher. Kosher salt contains no additives, unlike table salt, which can contain iodine and dextrose (sugar). I prefer my salt to be pure and free of additives, which makes for a more refined salty taste. Kosher also has significantly larger crystals than other salts, so a measure or pinch of it tastes less salty.

When it comes to brands, Diamond Crystal is my choice—probably because every restaurant I ever worked at had their iconic red box sitting on the shelf, which is a good stamp of approval. The other major producer of kosher salt is Morton, which has smaller and denser crystals compared to the larger, flakier crystals of Diamond Crystal. There is great debate in the culinary world about these two brands, but overall, you'll find that due to the difference in crystal size, Morton more densely packs into a measuring spoon compared to Diamond Crystal. This means that if you use the same volume of each salt, Morton's will be saltier than Diamond Crystal. Because all the recipes in this book were tested using Diamond, you may need to adjust your seasoning if you're using Morton.

SPICES: Always keep ground spices in airtight containers and use them up within 6 months after purchase (once they've lost their aroma, their time in your pantry has, sadly, come to an end and it's time to replace them). I suggest buying ground spices in the bulk aisle and buying only the amount you need, especially if it's for a recipe you know you won't make often.

VANILLA: Should always be pure, never imitation. For a more intense experience, try subbing vanilla extract with vanilla bean paste in desserts that are a bit more complex.

VINEGARS: I love the punchy, puckery feel you get when vinegar touches your taste buds. A splash of vinegar can genuinely help to jazz up a recipe; whether it's in a dressing or a sauce, or used as a finisher, like when caramelizing onions as on page 85, vinegars can play an important role in how a dish tastes. I have a whole shelf in my pantry dedicated to oils and vinegars, and the vinegar side's population has increasingly gotten bigger in recent years. The standards are all there—distilled white, red and white wine, and balsamic—but also apple cider (which is used a lot in this book), malt, champagne, sherry, and rice among others. Quick note: rice wine vinegar comes in seasoned and unseasoned versions. Seasoned rice wine vinegar contains additives such as sugar and salt, and so the two should not be substituted for one another. You'll see lots of vinegar used in this book, so I encourage you to experiment with this often overlooked pantry staple.

The Classics

How could I write a book on sandwiches and not give a nod to the classics that have been around forever? In this chapter, some sandwiches get a bit of an update, while others are pretty true to the original incarnation that you'll know best. It was hard to pick which sandwiches would make the cut, and I did have to leave some out, but hey, there's always *The Book of Sandwiches 2*! I hope this chapter gets you into the groove of things and ready for what's to come in the rest of the book: an adventure in sandwich land. Enjoy every bite!

My Perfect Sandwich

TOMATO / SUN-DRIED TOMATO MAYO / SOURDOUGH

MAKES 4 SANDWICHES

SUN-DRIED TOMATO MAYO

½ cup mayonnaise

⅓ cup finely chopped sun-dried tomatoes

1 tsp cracked black pepper

ASSEMBLY

8 slices thick-cut sourdough, toasted

Red or green leaf lettuce

4 heirloom tomatoes, sliced thick

Kosher salt to taste

To me, nothing says summer quite like a toasted tomato sandwich. I included this in the Classics chapter because it was a staple in our house growing up. I grew up in Windsor located at the very southern tip of Ontario and right across the river from Detroit. Nearby is Leamington, the tomato capital of Canada (there's even a giant tomato by the side of the highway and it's where most of the ketchup in Canada is bottled!). So, you see, we take our tomatoes and toasted tomato sandwiches seriously. I've casually surveyed my friends and, shockingly, a toasted tomato sandwich is not as classic as I thought. But it remains here, forever a classic to me.

The smell and taste of an excellent toasted tomato sandwich will always remind me of my childhood. Growing up, my mom and dad had a big garden in the backyard, and the crop they grew the most was tomatoes. Lunch for us, during the long, hot summer months, was almost always toasted tomato sandwiches—sandwiches slathered with tangy mayo (which almost melted on the hot, toasty bread) and layered with thick-cut tomatoes, almost always just freshly picked from the garden. My brothers and I would be out in our backyard climbing trees, making forts, and playing with our pet rabbits when we would hear our mom call out: "LUNCHTIME!" We would run toward the house with anticipation, our stomachs growling with hunger. Feeding four growing boys daily is not easy, but luckily for my mom, she found a sandwich that we all agreed was perfect.

This iteration amps up the tomato quotient by adding a good amount of sun-dried tomatoes to the mayo. This adds a bit of salt and a bit of tang, and I think it's just right. This super-simple yet delicious sandwich comes together in minutes. I hope you enjoy it.

To make the sun-dried tomato mayo, in a bowl, mix the mayo and sun-dried tomatoes together. Season with pepper and set aside.

Lay your tomato slices on a cutting board and season with salt. To assemble, spread a generous amount of the mayo on one side of each slice of toasted sourdough. Place a few pieces of lettuce on the mayo to hold it in place, and top with as many slices of tomato as your mouth can handle! Close with the other slice of sourdough. Enjoy!

Grilled Cheese: 3 Ways

I would argue that the grilled cheese could comfortably be included in the top five most iconic sandwiches of all time, possibly even the top three. It has been around in some form since the early 1900s (or even earlier, as the ancient Romans are believed to have added cheese to bread and warmed it up), and grilled cheese has now cemented its place in the culinary world as not only a home-cook comfort-food fave but also a beloved fixture on restaurant menus worldwide. And it's one of my personal favorites. With its versatility and endless possibilities for flavor combinations, there's sure to be a grilled cheese version that can make everyone's mouth water.

I love grilled cheese too much not to include more than one option for you, so here are three variations (and if I'm being honest, a few other grilled cheese–type sandwiches pop up in other chapters of the book as well . . . I'm looking at you, pages 85, 125, and 130). Let me know which one is your favorite!

Mozzarella / Panko / Italian Bread

MAKES 4 SANDWICHES

ASSEMBLY

3 cups shredded mozzarella

8 slices Italian bread

⅓ cup all-purpose flour

3 large eggs, beaten

1 tsp kosher salt

1½ cups panko

Extra-virgin olive oil for frying

Flaky salt

Mozzarella in carrozza, a classic southern Italian street food, is a grilled cheese lover's dream. To make it, divide the mozzarella equally among four slices of the bread. Top with the remaining slices of bread and press down firmly.

Line a baking sheet with paper towel and set a wire rack overtop. You'll see this method used throughout the book whenever we're about to fry. Set out a dredging station of three bowls: one with the flour, the next with the beaten eggs and salt, and the last with the panko.

Carefully coat each sandwich in the flour, then dip it in the eggs, and then dip it in the panko.

Heat a cast-iron pan over medium heat and add enough oil to fill the pan about ¼ inch deep. Once the oil is glistening, carefully lay the sandwiches in the pan (one or two at a time, depending on the size of your pan) and fry for about 2–2½ minutes per side; you're looking for the panko to become golden brown and the cheese oozy and almost about to burst out. Remove the sandwiches from the pan, place on the wire rack, and finish with a sprinkling of flaky salt. Repeat with the remaining sandwiches. As with all sandwiches, but particularly with grilled cheese, serve immediately. Enjoy!

CONTINUED

Havarti / Provolone / Chicken / Honey Glaze / Sourdough

MAKES 4 SANDWICHES

HONEY GLAZE

⅓ cup runny honey

1 tbsp grainy mustard

1 tsp soy sauce

1 tsp hot sauce

CHICKEN

2 cups pulled roasted or rotisserie chicken

1 tbsp brown sugar

1 tsp onion powder

1 tsp garlic powder

1 tsp smoked paprika

1 tsp kosher salt

1 tsp cracked black pepper

ASSEMBLY

8 slices sourdough

½ cup mayonnaise

8 slices Havarti

8 slices provolone

Make the glaze by mixing the honey, mustard, soy sauce, and hot sauce in a small bowl. Set aside.

In a separate bowl, mix the chicken with the brown sugar and seasonings. Add to a large skillet over medium-high heat, warm slightly, and set aside.

Make two sandwiches at a time: spread two slices of sourdough with 1 tbsp each of the mayonnaise. Place the slices mayo side down in a large skillet over medium-low heat.

Build the sandwiches in the pan by placing two slices of Havarti on top of each slice of bread, followed by ½ cup of warmed pulled chicken and two slices of provolone. Close each sandwich with another slice of sourdough, press down firmly and cover the pan with a lid. Let the cheese slowly melt.

After about 6 minutes, the bottom of each sandwich will have started browning and the cheese will have begun to melt. Spread the top slices of bread with the remaining mayo and flip. Press down firmly and cover with the lid; let the other side start to brown and the cheese melt for another 6 minutes.

Once both sides have taken on some good color, brush the glaze on each side and flip a few times until golden brown on both sides and the cheese is melted and gooey. Finish by brushing the glaze on each side one more time, then remove from the pan. Repeat with the other two sandwiches. Enjoy!

Beaufort / Gorgonzola / Pear Jam / Walnut Bread

MAKES 4 SANDWICHES

CHEESE

1 cup grated Beaufort cheese

1 cup crumbled Gorgonzola

¼ cup crème fraîche

ASSEMBLY

½ cup mayonnaise

8 slices walnut bread

½ cup pear jam (like the one on page 167)

4 tbsp grainy mustard

In a mixing bowl, combine both kinds of cheese and the crème fraîche and mix well. Set aside.

Spread 1 tbsp of the mayo on one side of each slice of bread. Flip the bread and add a few tablespoons of jam to the other side of four of the slices. For the other four slices, add a tablespoon of mustard and about ½ cup of the cheese mixture to each. Sandwich one of the jam slices on each to make four sandwiches.

Heat a large nonstick pan over medium-low heat. Add two sandwiches at a time and cook for about 6–7 minutes, or until a golden-brown crust has developed. Flip, pressing down ever so gently to prevent the cheese from bursting out. Continue to cook for 6–7 minutes or until browned on both sides and the cheese oozes out. Repeat with the other two sandwiches. Enjoy!

Top & middle: Havarti / Provolone /
Chicken / Honey Glaze / Sourdough
Bottom: Beaufort / Gorgonzola /
Pear Jam / Walnut Bread

An Egg Salad Sandwich

EGG / ZA'ATAR DRESSING / HERB SALAD / MULTIGRAIN

MAKES 4 SANDWICHES

EGGS
8 large eggs

ZA'ATAR DRESSING
¼ cup mayonnaise
¼ cup Greek yogurt
Zest of 1 lemon
1 tbsp za'atar
½ tsp kosher salt (check if your za'atar has salt; if it does, omit the salt here)

HERB SALAD
¼ cup roughly chopped fresh dill
¼ cup roughly chopped fresh cilantro
⅓ cup picked fresh flat-leaf parsley leaves
¼ cup picked fresh tarragon
1 tbsp extra-virgin olive oil
Juice of 1 lemon
½ tsp kosher salt
1 tsp cracked black pepper

ASSEMBLY
½ cucumber, thinly sliced
8 slices thick-cut multigrain bread, toasted and buttered

An egg salad sandwich, that classic lunchtime favorite—or sometimes not so favorite if your mom packed it for your lunch when you were a kid and all the other kids would make fun of you for your smelly lunch. You know what I mean. The egg salad sandwich can get a bad rap and isn't always thought of with much reverence, but I'm here to change that.

I love za'atar, a Middle Eastern blend of herbs and spices that sometimes includes cumin, coriander, sumac, Aleppo pepper, and sesame seeds, although the blend does differ depending on the region of the Middle East. Paired with a fresh, bright dressing and a refreshing herb salad and some thinly sliced cucumber, this egg salad sandwich will most certainly *not* remind you of that sad-looking creation your mom used to send you to school with (sorry, Mom!).

Place the eggs in a large pot and cover with cold water. Bring the water to a rolling boil, cover, and turn off the heat. You're looking for hard-boiled eggs here, so keep them in the water for 12 minutes. Transfer the eggs to an ice bath to cool completely. Once cooled, peel the eggs and give them a very rough chop—no mushy eggs here!

To make the dressing, place the mayo, yogurt, lemon zest, za'atar, and salt (if using) in a medium bowl and mix until combined. Toss in the eggs and give them a gentle mix, just until they are well coated.

For the herb salad, combine the dill, cilantro, parsley, and tarragon in a bowl. Toss with the olive oil and lemon juice and season with salt and pepper.

To assemble, divide the cucumber slices and egg between four slices of toasted multigrain, and top with the herb salad. Close the sandwiches with the remaining slices of toasted multigrain and enjoy!

(BACON, LETTUCE & FRIED GREEN TOMATO SANDWICH, WITH A WICKED AVOCADO SPREAD TO BOOT—THANKS, JANETTE!)

The BLFGT

FRIED GREEN TOMATO / BACON / AVOCADO / LETTUCE / BRIOCHE

MAKES 4 SANDWICHES

BACON

8 slices thick-cut bacon

TOMATOES

1 cup all-purpose flour

1 tsp kosher salt

1 tsp cracked black pepper

½ tsp smoked paprika

1 large egg

½ cup buttermilk

2 tbsp hot sauce

1 cup cornmeal

½ cup finely grated parmesan

3–4 green tomatoes, sliced into ½-inch rounds

Avocado oil for frying

Flaky salt to finish

AVOCADO SPREAD

2 avocados, peeled and pitted

¼ cup Greek yogurt

2 tbsp chopped fresh cilantro

Juice of 1 lime

1 tsp kosher salt

½ tsp cracked black pepper

ASSEMBLY

4 brioche buns, toasted and buttered

½ small head romaine, shredded

It's the BLT's time to shine. A classic, for sure, but never the star of the show. A sort of sidekick, if you will, to the more robust club sandwich or the flashier Reuben. But I'm here to say that it's time the BLT got a little love and a much-deserved update. Here, we're swapping out the fresh tomatoes for fried green tomatoes because, well, fried green tomatoes! And that's not all; the traditional mayo is being swapped out for a fresh green avocado spread that I guarantee will take this sandwich all the way to the best-dressed list.

Position a rack in the top section of the oven, preheat the oven to 400°F, line a baking sheet with foil and place a wire rack on top.

If you've never cooked bacon in the oven before, you're in for a treat. This foolproof way keeps your stovetop free of grease splatters and allows you to do other things while the bacon crisps up in the oven. On the prepared baking sheet, arrange the bacon slices in one row—it's okay if they're touching slightly—and place in the hot oven for 18–20 minutes. This will give you perfectly cooked bacon that will be crispy but still leave a bit of chew, ideal for a sandwich. Set aside.

Set out three medium bowls. In the first one, combine the flour, salt, pepper, and paprika and give it a quick mix. In the second bowl, place the egg, buttermilk, and hot sauce and whisk until thoroughly combined. Finally, in the third bowl, toss together the cornmeal and parmesan.

Line a baking sheet with paper towels and set a wire rack overtop. Time to fry some green tomatoes. Heat about ½ inch of oil in a cast-iron pan or heavy-bottomed pot over medium heat until the oil begins to glisten.

To dredge the tomatoes, place a few slices in the flour and coat both sides. Dip into the egg mixture and finally into the cornmeal mixture, patting the cornmeal onto the tomato to ensure it sticks.

Fry the tomatoes in batches by adding three or four at a time to the pan. Fry for about 2- 3 minutes, then carefully flip and fry for 2- 3 more minutes, or until golden brown on both sides. Remove to the wire rack and sprinkle with flaky salt. Repeat until all the tomatoes are fried.

The avocado spread can be either smooth or chunky. Place all the ingredients in a mini or regular food processor and blitz until smooth. If you prefer something chunkier, place the ingredients in a bowl and mash with a fork until you reach your desired consistency.

To assemble, spoon a generous amount of avocado spread on the bottom of each bun, then top with fried tomatoes, bacon, and lettuce. Finish with the top of the bun.

33

My Reuben

MAPLE CORNED BEEF / RUSSIAN DRESSING / SAUERKRAUT / GRUYÈRE / MARBLE RYE

MAKES 4 SANDWICHES

MAPLE CORNED BEEF
1 lb (454 g) corned beef
¼ cup maple syrup

RUSSIAN DRESSING
½ cup mayonnaise
2 tbsp ketchup
1 large dill pickle, finely minced
1 tsp Worcestershire sauce
1 tsp hot sauce
1½ tsp creamed horseradish
Zest of 1 lemon
1 tsp sweet paprika
½ tsp dry mustard

SAUERKRAUT
1 tsp extra-virgin olive oil
1 cup sauerkraut, well drained and squeezed dry

ASSEMBLY
8 slices marble rye
8 slices Gruyère
Unsalted butter, softened
Pickles to serve

The Reuben, the classic American sandwich, has been around for over 100 years, and its origin story is, like a lot of other classic sandwiches, not cut and dried. Whether it was created in a deli in New York in the early 1910s or in Omaha, Nebraska, in the 1920s, it's been a staple of the lunch counter for a long time now.

Certain sandwiches don't need much tweaking, and I think the Reuben is one of them. With its silky smooth corned beef, vinegary sauerkraut, creamy Russian dressing, and sweet and salty Gruyère, there's a lot to love. But I wanted to take this classic diner sandwich and throw a little Canadiana into it, so I added maple syrup to the corned beef, which brings a bit of sweetness to the sandwich and counters the salty beef nicely. There are many recipes for Russian dressing out there, and I love this one so much that it appears in a few sandwiches in the book. I suggest you make a batch and keep it in the fridge for those unexpected late-night sandwich cravings.

In a mixing bowl, gently toss the corned beef and maple syrup. Set aside.

For the dressing, place everything in a mixing bowl and mix until fully incorporated. Set aside.

For the sauerkraut, heat the oil in a small pan over medium-high heat. Add the sauerkraut and sauté, stirring frequently—the sauerkraut will crackle, so keep an eye on it! Once warmed through, remove from the heat and set aside.

To assemble, lay out the slices of bread and generously slather one side of each slice with the dressing. Top four of the slices with a piece of Gruyère, some warmed sauerkraut, corned beef, and another slice of Gruyère. Close the sandwiches with the remaining slices of bread, and they're almost ready for the pan. Spread a bit of softened butter over the top slices of bread.

Heat a large cast-iron pan over medium heat. Add one sandwich, butter side down, and fry for about 3–4 minutes, until golden, pressing down firmly a few times. Before flipping, butter the top slice, then flip and continue to fry until the second side is golden and crisp and the cheese is melted.

Serve with pickles on the side.

 FUN FACT The "corn" in corned beef refers to the size of the salt crystals used for the curing process of the beef and has nothing to do with actual corn.

GRILLING SAUSAGES

When grilling sausages, indirect heat is critical. Grilling sausages directly over a high flame will cook the sausages too fast, triggering the fat and juices in them to heat up to the boiling point and causing the sausages to split and the juices to spray out. Not good. Here's how to grill your sausages the right way.

Make sure that your grill is clean before you begin to BBQ. Preheat one side of the BBQ to medium for about 10 minutes—you're aiming for the grill to reach about 350°F before you start cooking. Once the BBQ has reached temperature, add the sausages to the side of the grill that is *not* on (indirect heat). Cook for 10–12 minutes on this side with the lid closed, turning them every so often. Once they are nearly fully cooked, move the sausages to the other side of the grill (direct heat) to finish them with some beautiful charring and grill marks, a few minutes per side. You can test your sausages for doneness using an instant-read thermometer (you'll know they're done when it hits 160°F). Poking holes in freshly grilled sausages is not recommended, as it will cause them to burst, releasing all that good juice you just worked so hard at developing. Instead, I say use your best judgment and avoid ruptured, dry sausages. Now go get your grill on, you newly minted grill master!

Sausages on a Bun, 3 ways pages 38–39
Top left: Grilled Corn / Jalapeños / Cream Cheese / Hot Sauce
Bottom Left: Kimchi / Bacon / Mayo
Right: Blue Cheese / Hot Sauce / Celery

Sausage on a Bun: 3 Ways

RECIPE PHOTOS ON PAGE 36

Sausages are one of my favorite things to grill in the summer. Many butchers make excellent sausages, with flavors like sriracha, honey mustard, bacon, pesto, potato, and the list goes on. If you don't have access to these endless flavor combinations, I'm here to help you. We're using plain sausages and upping our toppings game here.

Some might question whether a sausage in a bun (or a hotdog for that matter) is indeed a sandwich. I revert to what I said earlier in the book: something between two slices of bread constitutes a sandwich. And yes, technically, a bun is one piece of bread cut almost in half, but let's give this a pass, okay?

Grilling sausages, in my opinion, is the best way to cook them. But I think most people don't know the proper way to cook them, and therefore they tend to split open and end up dry. I've laid out my perfect grilling technique on page 37. One other key to a great sausage on a bun is a toasted bun. Once the sausages are grilled, toss the buns on the grill, cut side down, for a few minutes or until they reach the desired toasty-ness!

Sausage / Kimchi Mayo / Bacon / Bun

MAKES 4 SANDWICHES

ASSEMBLY

1 cup kimchi, squeezed dry and roughly chopped, liquid reserved

⅓ cup mayonnaise

4 toasted sausage buns

4 grilled sausages (see page 37)

4 green onions, thinly sliced

4–6 slices bacon, cooked and chopped

Black and white sesame seeds for garnish

In a bowl, mix the reserved kimchi liquid with the mayonnaise. Slather the mayo onto both sides of the toasted buns and top each with a grilled sausage. Mound the kimchi on the sausages, scatter with green onions, and sprinkle with bacon bits. Garnish with sesame seeds. Enjoy!

Sausage / Blue Cheese Sauce / Hot Sauce / Bun

MAKES 4 SANDWICHES

BLUE CHEESE SAUCE

¼ cup sour cream

¼ cup mayonnaise

⅓ cup crumbled blue cheese

1–2 tbsp heavy cream (depending on how thick you want the sauce)

1 tsp cracked black pepper

ASSEMBLY

4 toasted sausage buns

4 grilled sausages (see page 37)

Handful of celery leaves

Hot sauce to taste

To make the blue cheese sauce, place everything in a bowl and mix until fully incorporated. Feel free to break up the blue cheese into small pieces or keep some larger chunks for a bit more texture. Cover and refrigerate until needed.

To assemble, slather the toasted buns with the blue cheese sauce and nestle a grilled sausage on top. Finish with a bit more blue cheese sauce, celery leaves, and as much hot sauce as your heart desires. Enjoy!

Sausage / Grilled Corn / Jalapeño / Cream Cheese / Bun

MAKES 4 SANDWICHES

CORN TOPPING

1 cup grilled corn kernels

1 jalapeño, seeded and finely minced (or keep the seeds in for a spicier experience)

2 green onions, thinly sliced

1 clove garlic, finely grated

3 oz (85 g) cream cheese, softened

¼ cup sour cream

Zest and juice of 1 lime

1 tbsp hot sauce (optional)

½ tsp kosher salt

½ tsp cracked black pepper

ASSEMBLY

4 grilled sausages (see page 37)

4 toasted sausage buns

To make the corn topping, in a bowl, combine the corn kernels, jalapeño, green onions, garlic, cream cheese, sour cream, lime zest and juice, hot sauce, and salt and pepper. Mix well.

To assemble, add the grilled sausages to the toasted buns and top with a generous amount of the corn mixture. Enjoy!

Muffuletta, page 42

Muffuletta

OLIVE SALAD / ITALIAN CURED MEATS / ITALIAN CHEESE / MUFFULETTA LOAF

MAKES 6–10 WEDGES

OLIVE SALAD

2 cups mixed olives, pitted and roughly chopped

½ cup chopped roasted red peppers

⅓ cup chopped oil-packed artichoke hearts

¼ cup capers, drained

½ red onion, thinly sliced

3 cloves garlic, finely minced

2 tbsp chopped fresh flat-leaf parsley

⅓ cup extra-virgin olive oil

3 tbsp red wine vinegar

1 tsp chili flakes

1 tsp dried oregano

1 tsp cracked black pepper

ASSEMBLY

1 large muffuletta loaf, or 1 large round rustic loaf, cut in half and somewhat hollowed out

7 oz (200 g) mortadella, thinly sliced

7 oz (200 g) spicy soppressata, thinly sliced

7 oz (200 g) provolone, sliced

7 oz (200 g) capocollo, thinly sliced

7 oz (200 g) prosciutto, thinly sliced

7 oz (200 g) mozzarella, sliced

RECIPE PHOTO ON PAGE 40

The muffuletta was not, as many people might believe, born in Italy. This sandwich's origin story dates back to 1906 at an Italian market named Central Grocery, in the French Quarter of New Orleans. The market's owner, an Italian immigrant named Lupo Salvatore, is credited with inventing the sandwich. The story goes that Sicilian farmers working at the local farmers' market would have lunch at his store and order olive salad, meats, cheeses, and bread, but eat them all separately. Signor Salvatore was the one to suggest it might be easier to eat them all together, and that is how the muffuletta was born.

The combination of briny, slightly salty olive salad paired with layers upon layers of cured meats and cheese is the perfect sandwich to share with friends. Or in my case, eat it alone over the course of a week while writing a cookbook on sandwiches. If you have any leftovers, don't worry; they're even tastier the next day as I can attest to.

To make the olive salad, combine everything in a large mixing bowl and mix well. Cover and refrigerate for at least an hour or overnight.

To assemble this beast, lay out the two halves of the muffuletta loaf and divide the olive salad between them. Pour any leftover liquid onto the salad-topped bread. Layer the other fillings for the sandwich on the bottom half, beginning with the mortadella and followed by the soppressata, provolone, capocollo, prosciutto, and finally the mozzarella.

Sandwich with the top half of the loaf and wrap tightly in plastic wrap. Place between two large baking sheets with a heavy weight on top. Pop it into the fridge for 4 hours or overnight, flipping the sandwich at the midway mark.

When ready to serve, remove from the fridge, unwrap, and slice into wedges. Enjoy!

Chicken Cutlet Club Sandwich

FRIED CHICKEN / HAM / TOMATO / ICEBERG / MAYO / WHITE BREAD

MAKES 4 SANDWICHES

CHICKEN

4 skinless, boneless chicken thighs

¼ cup cornstarch

2 tbsp all-purpose flour

1 tsp kosher salt

1 tsp cracked black pepper

2 large eggs

2 tbsp grainy mustard

1 tbsp hot sauce

2 cups panko

Neutral oil for frying, such as grapeseed or sunflower

ASSEMBLY

⅓ cup mayonnaise

12 slices white sandwich bread, toasted

¼ head iceberg lettuce, shredded

3 tomatoes, sliced

12 slices smoked ham

As far as classics go, this sandwich could possibly be elevated to icon status. It's on every diner's menu up and down both coasts of North America and everywhere in between. It's also one of the most recognizable sandwiches, with its iconic triangle cuts and layers of bread and fillings, usually turkey and bacon (we change that up here, but we'll get to that later).

But what is its origin story, you ask? The name is believed to come from the fact that it was a staple at clubhouses and private, members-only clubs in the late 1800s. A far cry from where it currently resides—talk about a glow-down (is that a thing?). Anyways, we're here to give it a much-deserved glow-up. Here, we're swapping out the sliced turkey for perfectly fried chicken strips. Yes, it changes the sandwich quite a bit, but sometimes change is good. Also, if you can't tell already, I love fried food and think it is the perfect addition to many sandwiches. I also replaced the bacon with smoky sliced ham. Hear me out: the fried chicken cutlets already bring lots of texture to the sandwich, and though I wanted to be faithful to the original by including bacon, I think sliced smoked ham just works better. The tomato and lettuce stay loyal to the original, and we're using good old plain mayo here, nothing fancy. I hope you enjoy it!

The goal for this sandwich is to have even, flat pieces of chicken. To do this, place the chicken thighs between two pieces of plastic wrap and use a meat mallet, rolling pin, or the bottom of a heavy-duty pan to pound the chicken until the pieces are about ¼ inch thick.

Prepare a dredging station. In a bowl, place the cornstarch, flour, salt, and pepper and stir to combine. In a second bowl, place the eggs, grainy mustard, and hot sauce and whisk to combine. Finally, place the panko in a third bowl.

Heat about ½ inch of oil in a heavy-bottomed pot or cast-iron pan over medium-high heat. While the oil is heating, dredge the chicken by placing it in the cornstarch mixture first, then giving it a shake before dipping it into the egg mixture. Finally, place the chicken in the panko and press the crumbs into the cutlet to ensure maximum coverage.

CONTINUED

Line a baking sheet with paper towels and set a wire rack on top. Carefully lay two cutlets in the hot oil and fry for about 3–5 minutes per side, at which point they'll be nicely browned and cooked through. You'll know the cutlets are done when an instant-read thermometer reads 165°F when inserted into the thickest part of the cutlet. Remove to the wire rack and sprinkle with salt. Repeat with the remaining chicken. Once all the cutlets are fried and have cooled slightly, cut them into thick strips.

To assemble each sandwich, spread a generous amount of mayo on three slices of toasted bread. Top one with a handful of shredded lettuce and some chicken strips, then add another slice of the toasted bread, mayo side up. A few slices of tomato go on next, topped with a few slices of ham. Finally, top with the third slice of toasted bread, mayo side down. Repeat to build the other sandwiches. If you're feeling nostalgic, cut into triangles. Enjoy!

Did you know that some people say that the word "CLUB" in "Club Sandwich" stands for "Chicken Lettuce Under Bacon"? I know. My mind was blown too! Thanks to my friend Zeke (whose lovely hands hold some of the sandwiches in this book) for this little bit of sandwich trivia!

A Tuna Melt Sandwich

TUNA / MISO / WHITE CHEDDAR / SOURDOUGH

MAKES 4 SANDWICHES

TUNA

3 (6 oz/170 g) cans oil-packed tuna, well drained

½ cup mayonnaise

2 tbsp white miso

1 tsp hot sauce (optional)

½ tsp ground ginger

2 stalks celery, diced

¼ cucumber, diced

2 green onions, finely chopped

¼ cup finely chopped fresh flat-leaf parsley

Zest and juice of ½ lemon

1 tsp kosher salt

ASSEMBLY

8 slices sourdough, toasted and buttered

2 cups shredded old white cheddar

I could not wait to write, test, and taste this sandwich as soon as I knew I was writing this cookbook. I love a tuna melt like Taylor Swift loves a good breakup. Something to sink your teeth into, you know? This recipe is pretty simple to make but packs a punch and will satisfy that craving. What craving, do you ask? Well, that craving for a tuna melt, of course. You wouldn't still be reading this intro if you didn't love tuna melts as much as I do, now, would you?

To make my version of a tuna melt unique, I've added miso to the mix to intensify the flavor. The melted white cheddar ups the umami-ness of the sandwich, and the chewy, tangy sourdough brings it all together. I eat this sandwich while listening to one of Taylor's breakup ballads, but don't worry, the crying's not from the sandwich.

This is one of the quicker recipes in the book. Are you ready? Here we go!

In a large mixing bowl, combine the tuna, mayonnaise, miso, hot sauce (if using), ground ginger, celery, cucumber, green onions, parsley, lemon zest and juice, and salt. Mix well until thoroughly combined.

Turn the oven to broil and line a baking sheet with foil.

Place four of the toasted and buttered sourdough slices on the prepared baking sheet and divide the tuna mixture evenly among them. Top the mixture with even amounts of cheese. Pop the baking sheet under the broiler for about 2 minutes, or until the cheese is melted and bubbling. Remove from the oven and top each with another slice of toasted, buttered sourdough. Dig in and enjoy!

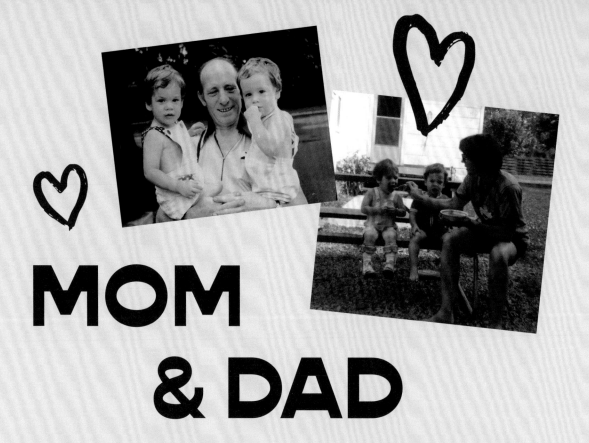

MOM & DAD

The peanut butter and jam sandwich hits home for me, as it is a symbol, in a way, of my parents. You see, my mom was known for making her own peanut butter. It was an almost twice-a-week tradition for her—we ate a lot of peanut butter in our house (four boys and a husband). The image of her standing at the kitchen counter with her old Oster blender, adding peanuts she had just roasted in the oven, is ingrained in my mind. I loved being in the kitchen with her; whether I was helping or not, I just loved being next to her while she cooked. There was a joy we would have when she finished jarring the peanut butter and handed us the blender and spatula to lick, like other mothers would do with mixing bowls stained with cake batter. I still eat lots of peanut butter, and every time I make a fresh batch, I think of her and that old Oster blender.

As I've said before in this book, Mom was a bit ahead of her time when it came to health food and healthy eating. She was also far ahead of the trend in using milk powder to enhance flavor; although in this case I think she was adding it to the peanut butter to inject us with some calcium, as we were not a milk-drinking household. I've

kept her peanut butter recipe exactly as she used to make it; I just wish I had that old Oster blender to complete the experience!

My dad adopted the title of jam maker later in his life. He absolutely loved coming up with new flavors and spending hours in the kitchen while his jams sat on the stovetop, boiling away. The scent of the cooking fruit would fill the house, and my mom was happy that she wasn't the one stuck in the kitchen. As the kids slowly left the house to join the working world, the roles in my parents' house flipped. My dad was the one who spent most of the time in the kitchen and my mom happily stepped away.

There was never a trip to Mom and Dad's without a trip to the garage, where Dad would store the cases upon cases of jams he had made. He was so proud of these jars of jam, and we were always so excited to be able to bring them home. He made so much jam that we would share them with friends and colleagues. My nieces lovingly referred to it as "Grandpa's Jam." I bet if I were to look in some of my brothers' fridges, there might still be a jar or two lingering around—unopened, of course.

For Mom & Dad

PEANUT BUTTER / BLUEBERRY CHIA JAM / WHITE BREAD

MAKES 4 SANDWICHES (ABOUT 2 CUPS JAM & 4 CUPS PEANUT BUTTER)

PEANUT BUTTER

3 cups dry-roasted unsalted peanuts

¼ cup instant skim milk powder

Pinch of kosher salt

BLUEBERRY CHIA JAM

6 cups frozen blueberries

½ cup maple syrup

Zest and juice of 2 limes

1½ tsp ground cardamom

3 tbsp chia seeds

ASSEMBLY

8 slices white bread

RECIPE PHOTO ON PAGE 49

Simple, straightforward peanut butter and jam sandwich. You didn't think I would write a sandwich book and not include one of the most iconic sandwiches on the planet, did you? Well, I thought about it, but I know two people who would have been very annoyed that it did not make an appearance.

Let's start with the peanut butter. Place the peanuts in a food processor and run on high for about 20 seconds; you're looking for the peanuts to be chopped into small pieces. Remove ½ cup of the chopped peanuts—be careful of that blade!—and set them aside. Add the milk powder to the remaining peanuts and continue to process on high until smooth, about 3 minutes. Once smooth, scrape into a bowl and gently fold in the reserved peanut pieces and the salt. Set aside. Any leftover peanut butter can be stored in airtight containers in the fridge for up to 3 months.

To make the jam, place the blueberries in a medium saucepan over medium-high heat. Cook, stirring frequently, until the berries begin to break down and release some of their juice, about 5–6 minutes. Use a potato masher to smash the blueberries slightly, then add the maple syrup, lime zest and juice, and cardamom and bring to a boil. Reduce the heat to low and let the mixture simmer away for about 10 minutes. Remove from the heat, add the chia seeds, and stir. Let cool to room temperature.

Store the jam in jars. It can be kept in the fridge for up to 2 weeks or in the freezer for up to a year.

To assemble, spread a generous amount of peanut butter on one side of four slices of bread and a generous amount of jam on the other four slices. Sandwich together, cut on a diagonal, and enjoy!

Fresh Falafel

FALAFEL/ BABA GHANOUSH / YOGURT & FETA SAUCE / HOMEMADE PITA

MAKES 4 FALAFELS

PITA

1 tsp active dry yeast

½ cup warm water (about 105°F)

½ tsp granulated sugar

1½ cups all-purpose flour

1 tsp extra-virgin olive oil

1 tsp kosher salt

BABA GHANOUSH

2 large eggplants

Extra-virgin olive oil

Kosher salt and cracked black pepper

⅓ cup tahini

Zest and juice of 1 lemon

2 cloves garlic, finely grated

1 tsp kosher salt

½ tsp ground cumin

½ tsp smoked paprika

2 tbsp extra-virgin olive oil

FALAFEL BALLS

1 cup dried chickpeas, soaked overnight and drained

½ small red onion, roughly chopped

2 cloves garlic

1 cup roughly chopped fresh flat-leaf parsley

½ cup roughly chopped fresh cilantro

½ cup roughly chopped fresh mint

1 tsp kosher salt

1 tsp ground cumin

1 tsp smoked paprika

½ tsp ground cardamom

½ tsp cracked black pepper

1 tsp baking powder

Neutral oil for frying, such as grapeseed or sunflower

The falafel has gone global. It can be found everywhere, from the streets of Sydney to the cities of Germany, from markets in Lima to food trucks in the UK, and everywhere in between. There are disputes about the true origin of falafel, although most believe it was developed in Egypt sometime in the early 1900s. It has become a global superstar in the culinary world, and I wanted to include it in this book.

As you'll see elsewhere, I'm a big fan of eggplant and wish more people didn't have such an aversion to it. Although it may not be a vegetable you want to eat raw, it becomes soft, rich, and very creamy when roasted. I'm not lying when I say I usually have a batch of this baba ghanoush in the fridge—it's not only great on this falafel but beautiful as a dip for veggies, whether raw or grilled.

First we'll tackle the homemade pita. Combine the yeast, warm water, and sugar in a mixing bowl and let it sit for 5 minutes, until everything has become frothy. Add the flour, olive oil, and salt. Mix the dough in the bowl until it just starts to come together. Turn out onto a lightly floured work surface and knead until smooth. Return it to the bowl, cover, and let rest for 30 minutes.

Remove the rested dough from the bowl, return it to the lightly floured work surface, and knead again for 4–5 minutes. Place in a new, clean, oiled bowl, cover, and let rest in a warm place for 1 hour, or until doubled in size.

Preheat the oven to 500°F. Turn the dough out onto the lightly floured work surface, divide it into four pieces, and form them into equal-sized balls. Using a rolling pin, roll out each ball into a circle about ¼-inch thick.

Oil a cast-iron pan with olive oil. Place the pan in the pre-heated oven and let the pan heat up for 5 minutes. Open the oven door and carefully place one of the circles of dough on the heated pan. Bake for 3–4 minutes. Remove from the pan and repeat with the other dough circles until all the pitas are baked. The pita will keep for about 2–3 days in an airtight container, although they are best if eaten fresh.

Next, let's make the baba ghanoush. Keep the oven at 500°F and line a baking sheet with parchment paper. Cut the eggplants in half lengthwise, drizzle with a bit of olive oil, and season with salt and

CONTINUED

YOGURT & FETA SAUCE

½ cup Greek yogurt

2 tbsp crumbled feta

2 tbsp tahini

1 tbsp extra-virgin olive oil

½ tsp cracked black pepper

ASSEMBLY

4 tomatoes, sliced

¼ cucumber, thinly sliced

Pickled red onions (like those on page 183)

Picked fresh herbs, such as mint, dill, or parsley, for garnish

Hot sauce (optional)

pepper. Place the eggplant halves, cut side down, on the prepared baking sheet and roast in the oven for 30 minutes. Remove from the oven and set aside to cool.

Once the eggplants have cooled, scoop out the flesh from each half and discard the skin. Plop the flesh into a food processor or blender and add the tahini, lemon zest and juice, garlic, salt, cumin, paprika, and olive oil. Blend on high until smooth. Set aside. This recipe makes a generous amount of baba ghanoush; any leftovers can be stored in an airtight container in the fridge for up to 5 days.

For the falafel balls, place all the ingredients except the oil in a food processor and blend until thoroughly processed and smooth. Transfer to a mixing bowl and cover with a kitchen towel; the mixture will be somewhat wet, so place it in the fridge to chill and firm up for a minimum of an hour.

Line a baking sheet with paper towels and set a wire rack overtop. In a heavy-bottomed pot, heat 1 inch of oil to 350°F. Using your hands, divide the falafel mixture into 12–16 balls. Using a slotted spoon, carefully lower the balls into the hot oil a few at a time. Fry them for about 3–4 minutes, depending on the size of the balls, flipping them halfway through. The falafel balls should be nicely golden brown at this stage. Using the slotted spoon, remove them to the wire rack. Continue until the falafel balls are all fried. Once they are slightly cooled, crack into one and wonder in admiration of the beautiful green insides of your fluffy and fragrant falafels!

For the yogurt and feta sauce, place all the ingredients in a food processor and blend until smooth. If you find the sauce is too thick—I like mine to be able to drizzle easily—add splashes of water to thin it out until your desired consistency is reached.

To assemble, open each pita and spread a generous amount of the baba ghanoush all over the inside. Stuff with three or four balls, add a few slices of tomato and cucumber, drizzle with yogurt and feta sauce, and top with pickled red onions, fresh herbs, and a bit of hot sauce (if you like). Enjoy!

NOTES

1. While you may be tempted to forgo soaking the chickpeas and use canned instead, don't. Canned chickpeas are already soaked and cooked, so most of their natural starch is gone and they have a much higher moisture content. Yes, it's one extra step, but you'll thank me when your falafel balls aren't falling apart. The starch in the dried chickpeas is what helps bind the falafel and prevent it from crumbling when fried.

2. This sandwich includes a recipe for homemade pita. We're all busy and I understand if you don't have time to make your own pita. Please feel free to use store-bought here instead.

The Steak Sandwich in This Book

GRILLED STEAK / ASPARAGUS PESTO / GARLIC BREAD

MAKES 4–6 SANDWICHES

STEAK

½ cup finely chopped fresh flat-leaf parsley

¼ cup extra-virgin olive oil

Zest and juice of 1 lemon

4 cloves garlic, minced

2 anchovy fillets, minced

1 tsp cracked black pepper

2 lb (900 g) (roughly) flank steak

ASPARAGUS PESTO

12–14 stalks asparagus, woody ends trimmed, roughly chopped

3 cloves garlic, roughly chopped

⅓ cup pistachios

1 cup finely grated pecorino

3 anchovy fillets

½ tsp chili flakes

⅓ cup extra-virgin olive oil

GARLIC BREAD

1 head garlic, tops cut off to expose the cloves

1 tbsp extra-virgin olive oil

1 tsp kosher salt

½ tsp cracked black pepper

½ cup unsalted butter, softened

½ cup finely grated pecorino

3 tbsp finely chopped fresh flat-leaf parsley

1 baguette, sliced in half lengthwise

RECIPE PHOTO ON PAGES 56 & 57

If you're a meat eater, you probably love a good steak sandwich. Grilled properly and served with the right accompaniments, it can be the perfect sandwich. For mine, I wanted to pair tender, juicy steak with something fresh and bright with a bit of umami: enter my asparagus pesto. It's a bit of a different take on pesto—gone is the traditional basil you might be used to and stepping into its place is raw fresh asparagus; pine nuts are swapped out for pistachios to bring a mild sweetness, and I've added anchovies. (Before you go running, let me explain why: Anchovies have a terrible reputation, one I firmly believe they do not deserve. Not only do they add some powerful umami to a dish, but the fishy taste that most people expect from them is almost entirely absent because of the curing process, which has them sitting in large vats of salt for up to 12 months.) All this to say that this pesto is delicious and will become best friends with your grilled steak. Plus, we're adding an incredibly easy garlic butter to spread onto your baguette, which will then be grilled. The butter becomes almost like a crown on a queen's head: it's the perfect way to finish this delicious sandwich. I hope you enjoy it.

First up, we'll marinate the steak. Place all the ingredients, except the steak, in a bowl and whisk. Place the steak in a resealable bag and pour in the marinade. Refrigerate for at least an hour or overnight.

Next up, let's make the asparagus pesto. Place the asparagus, garlic, pistachios, pecorino, anchovies, and chili flakes in a food processor. Process for 1–2 minutes, then, with the motor running, slowly pour the olive in through the chute. Continue to process until relatively smooth. Set aside. Any leftover pesto can be stored in an airtight container in the fridge for up to a week.

Preheat the oven to 350°F.

Now, prepare the garlic butter for the bread. Place the garlic bulbs on some foil, drizzle with olive oil, and season with salt and pepper. Wrap the foil tightly around the garlic and place on a baking sheet, then into the oven for 40 minutes. Remove from the oven and let cool. Squeeze the roasted garlic into a mixing bowl and mash with a fork. Add the softened butter, pecorino, and parsley and mix well. Set aside.

Time to grill that flank steak. Oil the grill, turn the heat to high, and let the temperature rise to 450°F to 500°F. Remove the steak from the marinade, letting any excess marinade drip back into the bag, and pat dry. Place the steak on the BBQ and grill for about 4–5 minutes per side. If you're someone who loves their steak done to a specific temperature, use an instant-read thermometer and you'll never be guessing if it's ready (I use one a lot in this book, so maybe it's time to invest!). The method I've described above will give you a medium-rare steak, which, when the steak comes off the grill, should be at an internal temperature of 130°F and will rise to about 135°F after resting. For rare steak, remove the steak when it reaches 120°F and it will rise to about 125°F after resting. If you prefer your steak medium, remove it when it hits 140°F and it will rise to about 145°F after resting. I wouldn't recommend going over medium for flank steak, but if you insist, be careful not to go over 155°F, which will give you a medium well-done steak. Anything more than that is simply criminal.

Remove the steak from the BBQ, tent it with foil, and let it rest for at least 10 minutes before slicing. When slicing steak, you want to ensure that you cut it against the grain for a truly tender piece of meat. On a large piece of flank steak like this one, finding the grain is fairly simple: You'll see parallel lines of muscle that run from one end of the steak to the other, and that is the grain. Slice against this (in other words, through the lines), starting at one corner, to create beautiful slices of steak—I like mine to be about ¼ to ½ inch thick, but feel free to make them thinner or thicker if that's your jam!

While the steak rests, make the garlic bread. Spread the prepared garlic butter on the cut side of each baguette and place cut side down on the hot side of the BBQ for about 30 seconds or until it's your desired toasty-ness.

To assemble, evenly distribute the steak over the bottom of the toasted garlic baguette and dollop it with the pesto. Top with the other half of the toasted baguette, slice, and serve.

FUN FACT

Lovingly known as the "smiling nut" in China, and the "happy nut" in Iran, pistachios, in fact, aren't nuts at all; they're seeds. And each pistachio tree produces about 50,000 of these tasty nuggets every 2 years.

breakfast

No sandwich book would be complete without a chapter devoted to and in praise of the mighty breakfast sandwich. It's an icon, ubiquitous, and the best hangover cure, and it's not going anywhere. But it is time to take it up a notch, change things up a little, and make her a bit more diverse. While one could argue that the mighty egg is most deserving of its place on the breakfast world's throne, plenty of others are keen to shine, and I'm here to give them their chance. I'm talking tahini granola and sautéed plums on sweet ricotta French toast; crunchy peanut butter, dark chocolate, caramelized bananas, and toasty sourdough; oh, and a wicked melted Taleggio, caramelized onion, cherry, and pistachio sandwich. See, no eggs in sight! Just kidding, there are plenty of eggs in this chapter, but I wanted to make sure we all remember that an egg does not a breakfast sandwich make.

Even though this chapter is titled "Breakfast," please do not be constrained by labels. Feel free to make the sandwiches in this chapter at the time of day that suits you best. Happy any-time-of-the-day breakfast sandwiching!

A Breakfast Burger

PORK PATTY / SPECK / CHEDDAR / FRIED EGG / AVOCADO / MAPLE MAYO / BRIOCHE

MAKES 4 BURGERS

MAPLE MAYO

½ cup mayonnaise

1 tbsp maple syrup

1 tbsp grainy mustard

1 tsp hot sauce

PORK PATTIES

1½ lb (680 g) ground pork

1 tbsp finely chopped fresh sage

½ tsp onion powder

½ tsp garlic powder

½ tsp kosher salt

1 tsp cracked black pepper

1 tbsp extra-virgin olive oil

ASSEMBLY

4 slices white cheddar

4 brioche buns, sliced and toasted

4 large eggs, fried

8 pieces speck, crisped

1 avocado, sliced

Flaky salt and cracked black pepper, to finish

Does a breakfast burger belong in the Burger chapter or the Breakfast chapter? The Breakfast chapter won out because of the runny fried egg, the sweet maple syrup in the sauce, and the salty, crispy speck. But wherever it's placed, it's a great sandwich, and I love it so much.

Again, salty-sweet is winning the battle for our taste buds here. I should start a scorecard with checkmarks for every sandwich in this book with a salty-sweet element. If you want to make this and don't have or can't find speck, replace it with slices of good old bacon or even leftover ham (fried up, of course). What you're after is the saltiness of the pork paired with the sweet and spicy sauce and the most iconic breakfast sandwich ingredient of all time: a runny fried egg. Add to that some fresh, creamy avocado slices and melted white cheddar, and I guarantee you that this will become a new favorite in your house.

For the maple mayo, place all ingredients in a mixing bowl and whisk to combine. Set aside.

To make the burgers, combine the pork, sage, onion powder, garlic powder, salt, and pepper in a mixing bowl. Mix until well combined. Divide the mixture into four even portions and flatten them into patties.

Heat the oil in a cast-iron pan over medium-high heat. Cook the patties in the pan, flipping after about 4 minutes. Continue to cook the other side for another 3 minutes and then place a slice of cheese on top. Cover and continue to cook for an additional minute or so, or until the cheese has melted nicely.

To assemble, liberally spread some maple mayo on the top and bottom of each bun. Top with a patty, followed by two pieces of speck, a fried egg, a few pieces of avocado and a sprinkling of flaky salt and cracked black pepper. Enjoy!

NOTE
If you're curious about burger temperatures, I've included a handy guide on page 144.

Thanks, Mom!

PLUM / SWEET RICOTTA / TAHINI GRANOLA / FRENCH TOAST

MAKES 4 OPEN-FACED SANDWICHES

GRANOLA

3 cups rolled oats

1 cup shredded unsweetened coconut

1 cup slivered almonds

¼ cup ground flaxseeds

1 tsp ground ginger

1 tsp kosher salt

⅓ cup tahini

⅓ cup maple syrup

¼ cup coconut oil, melted

SWEET RICOTTA

1⅓ cups ricotta

¼ cup runny honey

Zest of 1 lemon

1 tsp vanilla extract

PLUMS

2 tbsp unsalted butter

2 tbsp dark brown sugar

1 tsp ground ginger

Zest and juice of 1 lemon

4–6 ripe plums, pitted and sliced

FRENCH TOAST

4 large eggs

⅓ cup whole milk

1 tsp vanilla extract

Pinch of kosher salt

2 tbsp unsalted butter

4 thick slices brioche bread

ASSEMBLY

Maple syrup

My mom spent much time in the kitchen while we were growing up. Making her own yogurt, preserves, peanut butter, and bread—not to mention dinner for a family of six every night—the woman was busy! And if you've not guessed already, I give her much (if not the most) credit for my love of cooking and being in the kitchen—although by the time all the kids had left the coop, she was done with being in the kitchen. She manifested a new life for herself, and we were all so proud of her for making that happen. She opened a little health food store and ran that for almost 20 years. It wasn't always easy, but it had been her dream for a long time, showing you that you're never too old to make your dreams come true.

Opening that health food store was a culmination of years of reading and researching what were then (in the early 1970s) fringe movements in the culinary world—vegetarianism and health food. I will always say it: the woman was ahead of her time, and she instilled these food values in us, her kids. One of my favorite things she made was her granola. I've amended her recipe a bit here to suit this open-faced sandwich. This granola is quick and easy, and I now have a jar of it on my counter at all times—it makes for a great snack too!

We'll start with the granola. Preheat the oven to 300°F and line a baking sheet with parchment paper.

In a large bowl, combine the oats, coconut, almonds, flaxseed, ground ginger, and salt.

In a small bowl, whisk together the tahini, maple syrup, and coconut oil. Pour the tahini mixture over the oat mixture, toss to coat, and transfer to the prepared baking sheet. Bake for 40 minutes, mixing the granola halfway through. Set aside to cool while you make the ricotta and plums. The granola can be stored in an airtight container for a couple of weeks—although it probably won't last that long!

For the sweet ricotta, spoon the ricotta into a fine-mesh sieve placed over a bowl to drain for 20 minutes. Once drained, transfer to a medium bowl and gently mix in the honey, lemon zest, and vanilla. Cover and refrigerate until needed.

For the plums, melt the butter in a medium pan over medium-high heat. Add the sugar, ginger, and lemon zest and juice and stir until fully incorporated and the sugar has melted. Add the plums and sauté for 5–6 minutes; they won't take long to soften. Set aside.

We're almost there! It's French toast time, and then we can assemble the sandwich. In a large bowl, whisk together the eggs, milk, vanilla, and salt.

Melt 1 tbsp butter in a large nonstick pan over medium-high heat. Dunk two slices of brioche into the egg mixture, let soak for a minute or two and then place in the heated pan. Cook for 3 to 4 minutes per side or until nicely browned. Cover the French toast to keep it warm while you melt the remaining 1 tbsp butter in the pan and repeat with the other slices of brioche.

To assemble, place a slice of French toast on a plate. Spread a few dollops of ricotta on the toast and top with the plum slices and a scattering of granola. Drizzle with maple syrup and enjoy!

The Originator

FRIED EGG / CHORIZO / CRISPY KALE / SPICY HONEY BUTTER / ITALIAN BREAD

MAKES 4 SANDWICHES

CRISPY KALE

1 bunch purple kale, stems removed and leaves torn into pieces

1 tbsp extra-virgin olive oil

1 tsp kosher salt

SPICY HONEY BUTTER

⅓ cup unsalted butter

½ tsp sweet paprika

½ tsp cayenne

2 tbsp runny honey

Pinch of kosher salt and cracked black pepper

CHORIZO

2 chorizo sausages, casings removed

ASSEMBLY

8 slices Italian bread, toasted

4 large eggs, fried in extra-virgin olive oil

4 tbsp finely grated parmesan

Years ago, while in the UK, I stumbled upon this cute little café and decided to have breakfast. They served kale chips as a side, so I ordered them with my breakfast sandwich. When the food arrived, I thought, "Those kale chips would be a great addition to that sandwich." My brain started doing its thing, and before I had finished my breakfast, the idea for this sandwich was born. For a while I was making this at least once a week. I hope you do as well.

The crispy kale is a perfect addition to any sandwich and works beautifully with all the other flavors and textures in this particular one. Crispy kale is super easy to make, and feel free to play around with different types of kale. I call for purple kale, but honestly, any variety would be delicious.

A variation on the spicy honey butter pops up in another recipe in this book (see page 100). The idea is the same in both: creamy butter, sweet honey, and a bit of heat marry beautifully to create a quick "sauce" that you can keep in the fridge and use on other things like toast or waffles.

For the crispy kale, preheat your oven to 325°F and line a baking sheet with parchment paper. Place the kale pieces in a large mixing bowl and massage with olive oil and salt. Arrange the pieces on the prepared baking sheet, making sure not to overcrowd, so the kale does not steam. Bake for 10 minutes or until crisp.

While the kale crisps up in the oven, make the spicy honey butter. Combine the butter, paprika, cayenne, honey, salt, and pepper in a small pot over medium-high heat. Let the butter melt and whisk until beautifully combined. Set aside.

For the chorizo, heat a medium pan over medium-high heat. Add the chorizo and break up with a wooden spoon. Cook for about 6 minutes, or until nicely browned and cooked through.

To assemble, brush some of the spicy honey butter on one side of each slice of toast. Top four of the slices with a handful of crispy kale, a fried egg, some chorizo, and a sprinkling of grated parmesan. Drizzle a bit more of the honey butter on top and then close the sandwiches with the remaining slices of toast.

FUN FACT

I named this sandwich "The Originator" because it was the first thing Séb and I ever shot together many years ago—long before a cookbook on sandwiches was ever in the cards!

Croque Madame

JAMBON DE PARIS / FRIED EGG / HERB BÉCHAMEL / TOMATO / SOURDOUGH

MAKES 4 SANDWICHES

FRESH HERB BÉCHAMEL

4 tbsp unsalted butter

1 large or 2 small shallots, finely minced

2 cloves garlic, finely grated

4 tbsp all-purpose flour

2 cups buttermilk

½ tsp lemon juice

⅓ cup finely chopped fresh dill and chives

1½ tsp Dijon mustard

1 tsp kosher salt

½ tsp cracked black pepper

ASSEMBLY

8 slices sourdough, thinly sliced and lightly toasted

12 slices thinly sliced jambon de Paris or smoked ham

8 thin slices tomato

2 cups shredded Comté or Gruyère

4 large eggs, fried

Fresh herbs for garnish

NOTE

What is a roux? A roux is a mixture of equal parts flour and fat (in this case, butter), combined and cooked and used as a thickening agent.

The croque monsieur and the croque madame are legends in France and have also managed to travel onto menus worldwide. As with most sandwich origin stories, there are many versions for these. What we know for sure is that the croque monsieur was the first of the two to find its way onto menus in Paris. The earliest mention of it is in an article in *Le Journal Quotidien* dated May 17, 1893. It was referred to as "Le Croque-Monsieur Béarnaise," indicating that it may have originally been served with béarnaise sauce instead of the béchamel it is served with today. It's hard to know when exactly the croque madame made its debut on the scene, but there are mentions of it as early as 1932. It's thought that it got its name from the addition of the fried egg on top, said to be reminiscent of a lady's hat.

All this to say that it's is a rich, creamy, hearty sandwich, sure to satisfy you and whoever is lucky enough to have it served to them. Bon appétit!

Let's start by making the béchamel. Melt the butter in a medium pot over medium heat. Add the shallots and garlic and sauté for 1 minute. Add the flour and whisk until thoroughly combined and a roux has formed (see note). Slowly pour in the buttermilk and whisk constantly until the sauce has smoothed and thickened, about 3–4 minutes. Remove from the heat and stir in the lemon juice, herbs, Dijon, and salt and pepper. Set aside.

Preheat the oven to 425°F and line a baking sheet with parchment paper.

Place four slices of toasted sourdough on the prepared baking sheet and divide the majority of the béchamel and spread over each, ensuring end-to-end coverage. Place three pieces of ham on each slice and top with two slices of tomato. Sprinkle with half the cheese, then top with the remaining slices of toasted sourdough. Spread the tops of the sandwiches with the remaining béchamel and sprinkle with the remaining cheese. Bake in the oven until the cheese bubbles, about 5–6 minutes. Finish the sandwich by broiling for 1 minute or until nicely browned and bubbly.

Remove from the oven and let cool for a few minutes. Place each croque on a plate, top with a fried egg, and garnish with fresh herbs. Dig in and enjoy! You might also want to take a nap after this one— just a friendly warning!

Le Séb

CARAMELIZED BANANA / PEANUT BUTTER / DARK CHOCOLATE / SOURDOUGH

MAKES 4 SANDWICHES

BANANAS

3 tbsp unsalted butter

⅓ cup dark brown sugar

1 tsp ground cinnamon

4 bananas, peeled and halved lengthwise

ASSEMBLY

4 tbsp unsalted butter, softened

8 slices sourdough

1 cup crunchy or smooth peanut butter (store-bought or see the recipe on page 50)

⅓ cup finely chopped or grated dark chocolate

Flaky salt

Can we talk for a minute about how pretty this image is? Séb came up with the idea of shooting this as a prep shot because it shows you the sandwich's elements beautifully before it gets grilled and smooshed together. It quickly became one of Séb's favorite images, so I decided I needed to name it after him, and he's now obliged to eat this sandwich every week for the rest of his life. Have fun, Séb!

All kidding aside, I love this image so much. Lots of breakfast-table icons are present here: bananas, peanut butter, and chewy, tangy sourdough. And I've added dark chocolate because the sandwich was screaming for it when I tested it (and I'm glad it screamed at me, because chocolate is the perfect finisher here). Oh, and even though this sandwich appears in the Breakfast chapter, feel free to make it whenever you're craving something a little sticky and sweet. Bon appétit, mes amis.

We'll start with the bananas. Heat a large nonstick skillet over medium-high heat and add the butter. Let the butter melt and then add the sugar and cinnamon. Whisk until the sugar has dissolved, then add the bananas, cut side down. Let the bananas cook undisturbed for about 3 minutes, then very carefully flip and cook for 3 minutes more. If they happen to break when you flip them, that's okay; they're going to get smooshed into a sandwich in the end anyway! Remove from heat.

To assemble the sandwich, butter one side of each slice of sourdough and then flip and spread a generous amount of peanut butter, about 2 tbsp per slice, to the other side. Carefully top half the slices with two caramelized banana halves each, a sprinkling of chopped chocolate, and a tiny bit of flaky salt. Close the sandwich, buttered side out.

Heat a clean nonstick pan over medium heat. Once the pan is hot, add two sandwiches at a time and cook until the bread is nicely toasty and browned. Flip the sandwiches and cook until the second side is browned and the chocolate has melted. Remove from the heat and repeat with the remaining two sandwiches. Slice and enjoy!

Pastrami Monte Cristo

PASTRAMI / DIJON / GRUYÈRE / BLACK CHERRY / EGG BREAD

MAKES 2 SANDWICHES

ASSEMBLY

2 tbsp Dijon mustard

4 slices egg bread

2 tbsp mayonnaise

12 slices pastrami

4 slices Gruyère

4 tbsp black cherry jam

2 large eggs

Kosher salt and cracked black pepper

4 tbsp unsalted butter

I spend a lot of time in the UK, and when I'm in London, one of my favorite places to spend a Saturday morning is Borough Market. It bustles with people and teems with butchers, fishmongers, cheese makers, and spice traders. Not only can you get all your groceries from local purveyors, but there is an endless amount of takeout food stalls, with offerings from freshly shucked oysters and a glass of Champagne (be prepared, the lineups for oysters are always the longest) to paella, falafel, raclette, and much more—make sure you arrive with a healthy appetite.

The idea for this sandwich came about when my friends and I stopped at the market one Saturday morning and had breakfast. My pick was a duck pastrami Monte Cristo. It was a delight. I would have loved to include duck pastrami in this recipe, but it's simply much too hard to find; if you can find it, though, or better yet, if you can make it, go ahead and include it! This sandwich comes together quite quickly and would be great not only for a weekend brunch but also for a weeknight dinner.

Preheat the oven to 350°F and line a baking sheet with parchment paper.

Spread mustard over one side of two slices of the bread and mayonnaise over one side of the other two. Divide the pastrami between the two mustard-slathered slices and top each with two slices of Gruyère. Evenly spread a few tablespoons of black cherry jam over each and then top with the other slice of bread mayo side down.

Crack the eggs into a large bowl and season with salt and pepper. Whisk to combine.

Melt the butter in a cast-iron pan over medium heat. Carefully dip each sandwich into the egg mixture, letting each side soak for a minute or so, and then fry until the bottom is nicely golden brown, about 1–2 minutes. Flip and continue to cook for another 1–2 minutes.

Transfer the sandwiches to the prepared baking sheet and into the oven to melt the cheese, about 5 minutes. Remove from the oven and let the sandwiches rest for 5 minutes before digging in and enjoying!

Simply Bougie

OMELET / SMOKED SALMON / CRÈME FRAÎCHE / CAVIAR / TARRAGON / BRIOCHE

MAKES 2 SANDWICHES

CRÈME FRAÎCHE

4 tbsp crème fraîche

Zest of ½ lemon

OMELET

4 large eggs

½ tsp kosher salt

1½ tbsp unsalted butter

ASSEMBLY

2 brioche buns, toasted and buttered

2 oz (50 g) smoked salmon

2 tsp caviar

Fresh tarragon for garnish

Although pretty simple to make, this breakfast sandwich is a stunner! And quite bougie with the addition of the caviar, I must say. It comes together relatively quickly, but once it's brought to the table, your guests will be mighty impressed. If caviar is difficult to find or you don't want to fork out the money for it, you can substitute it with salmon roe, which is easily found at most grocery stores. And if you're having a hard time finding crème fraiche, you can substitute sour cream. Either way, you're getting a soft, savory, fresh sandwich that will most definitely wake up those taste buds.

For the crème fraîche, place it in a bowl and fold in the lemon zest. Set aside.

Next, let's whip up the eggs. Crack the eggs into a medium mixing bowl. Add the salt and whisk vigorously for a good minute or so—you want to ensure that the eggs are well combined.

Time to make the omelet: Melt the butter in a large nonstick pan over medium-heat. Once it has melted and is bubbly, add the eggs and swirl and shake the pan so all the egg travels to meet the hot pan. Let the egg cook until the bottom begins to set but the top is still slightly runny. To prevent any uncooked egg from pooling in the center, use a silicone spatula to lift the edges of the omelet and allow any uncooked egg to kiss the pan. Continue to do this until the omelet is fully set. Using your handy silicone spatula, fold the omelet over itself in the pan and then slide it onto a cutting board.

To assemble, add half the omelet to the bottom of each buttered bun and top with half of the salmon. Spoon half of the crème fraîche atop the salmon and finish with a teaspoon of caviar and a sprinkling of tarragon. Enjoy!

The "Geoff Wanted Me to Name a Sandwich after Him" Sandwich

FRIED CHICKEN / SPICY MAPLE SYRUP / SAVORY WAFFLE

MAKES 4 SANDWICHES

CHICKEN

1½ cups buttermilk

2 tbsp Buffalo-style hot sauce

2 tbsp pickle juice

4 skin-on, boneless chicken thighs (see note, page 76)

1½ cups all-purpose flour

⅓ cup cornstarch

1 tsp smoked paprika

1 tsp onion powder

1 tsp garlic powder

1 tsp baking powder

1 tsp kosher salt

1 tsp cracked black pepper

8 cups neutral oil for frying, such as grapeseed or sunflower

Flaky salt

WAFFLES

2 cups all-purpose flour

1 tbsp granulated sugar

4 tsp baking powder

1 tsp kosher salt

2 large eggs

1½ cups whole milk

6 tbsp melted unsalted butter

2 tbsp finely chopped fresh flat-leaf parsley

SPICY MAPLE SYRUP

1 cup dark maple syrup

2 tbsp Buffalo-style hot sauce

1 tsp cracked black pepper

ASSEMBLY

Fresh herbs, such as flat-leaf parsley, tarragon, or dill, roughly chopped

If you're looking for an origin story for chicken and waffles, you need to go back to Harlem in the 1930s during the jazz era, to a club called Dickies Club and its owner, Dickie Wells. Wells's supper club was where the jazz set would head late into the night. The crowds would filter in between dinnertime and breakfast, so his idea for pairing fried chicken (dinner) and waffles (breakfast) was born. Rumor has it that Wells served the dish with a cup of coffee and a shot of bourbon—not a terrible brunch idea, if I say so myself.

This is not the only fried chicken in this book. Its big sister, the fried chicken sandwich with (not so) secret sauce and greens, appears on the cover (and on page 95). But this version, equally delicious in so many ways, is served with savory waffles and a spicy, peppery, pleasantly sweet sauce. That sauce sounds a lot like how I describe my trainer and friend Geoff, and is one of the reasons I named this sandwich after him, the other being the fact that he loves fried chicken sandwiches. As with others who have sandwiches named after them, I'm sure he'll enjoy this one every weekend for the rest of his life. You're welcome, Geoff!

For the chicken, in a large mixing bowl, whisk together the buttermilk, hot sauce, and pickle juice. Place the chicken thighs into this marinade, cover, and refrigerate for at least 1 hour or, better yet, overnight.

Now it's dredging time: in a medium bowl, whisk together the flour, cornstarch, paprika, onion powder, garlic powder, baking powder, salt, and pepper.

Place wire racks on top of two baking sheets lined with paper towels (you'll use one now and one after the chicken is finished frying).

Remove the chicken from the fridge and, working with one thigh at a time, transfer from the buttermilk mixture, letting any excess marinade drip back into the bowl, to the flour mixture, ensuring that you have a good solid coating of flour. Place the dredged chicken on one of the wire racks.

Repeat this process until all four thighs are dredged and thoroughly coated in flour. Let the chicken air-dry on the rack for 15 minutes before frying. (Adding fridge-cold chicken to hot oil will reduce the temperature of the oil quickly; bringing it to room temperature helps ensure perfect crispy fried chicken.)

CONTINUED

75

Add the oil to a Dutch oven and heat to 350°F over medium-high heat.

Fry the chicken thighs, two at a time, in the hot oil for about 6–8 minutes, flipping every few minutes to ensure even browning. Once the chicken has reached an internal temperature of 165°F, it is ready. Transfer to the clean wire rack to drain off any excess oil, and sprinkle with flaky salt. Check the oil temperature and adjust the heat if necessary to keep it at 350°F, then repeat with the remaining thighs. Cover the fried chicken with foil until ready to assemble the sandwich.

Preheat a waffle iron (see note) and spray with nonstick baking spray.

In a large bowl, whisk together the flour, sugar, baking powder, and salt. In a separate bowl, whisk together the eggs, milk, melted butter, and parsley. Add the dry ingredients to the wet ingredients and stir to combine, but do not overmix.

Scoop ⅓ cup batter into the preheated waffle iron. Cook for about 2–3 minutes or until nicely browned and crisp; timing may vary depending on your waffle maker. Repeat until you have made 8 waffles.

Place the waffles on the wire rack with the fried chicken.

Meanwhile, for the spicy maple syrup, heat the maple syrup, hot sauce, and pepper in a small saucepan over medium-high heat and bring to a boil. Reduce the heat to low and let simmer until ready to pour.

To assemble, place a fried chicken thigh on a waffle, pour a generous amount of warmed spicy maple syrup over the chicken, sprinkle with herbs, and top with another waffle (or keep it as an open-faced sandwich, if you prefer). Feel free to spoon more maple syrup over the top of the sandwich. Enjoy!

NOTE

Skin-on, boneless chicken thighs are not the easiest to find. Substituting with skinless, boneless for this recipe is just fine. Or, see note on page 198 on how to easily debone a chicken thigh.

This recipe makes enough for eight 7-inch round waffles, but you can adjust accordingly for your size of waffle maker.

A Biscuit Breakfast

SMOKED TROUT / SAUCE GRIBICHE / BACON & CHIVE BISCUIT

**MAKES 4 SANDWICHES
(WITH LEFTOVER BISCUITS!)**

BISCUITS

2¼ cups all-purpose flour

1 tbsp baking powder

¼ tsp baking soda

1¼ tsp granulated sugar

1 tsp garlic powder

1 tsp kosher salt

½ cup fridge-cold unsalted butter, cubed

1½ cups shredded extra-old cheddar,

½ cup chopped crisped bacon (about 8 slices)

2 tbsp finely chopped fresh chives

1 cup chilled buttermilk + a bit more for brushing

Flaky salt

SAUCE GRIBICHE

2 tbsp Dijon mustard

2 tbsp grainy mustard

¼ cup extra-virgin olive oil

2 tbsp sherry vinegar

6 cornichons, diced

4 tbsp capers, roughly chopped

2 anchovy fillets, finely chopped

4 hard-boiled large eggs, roughly chopped

¼ cup chopped fresh flat-leaf parsley

2 tbsp chopped fresh tarragon

Cracked black pepper to taste

ASSEMBLY

10–12 oz (280–340 g) smoked trout

A few handfuls of arugula

I'm already jealous of how much attention this sandwich will inevitably get when the book comes out. And once you make it, I think you'll agree—this one is a stunner!

Very few recipes in this book include a recipe for the bread component. It was a conscious choice not to include bread recipes, because that's another book entirely. But a few sandwiches can only be enjoyed with a particular bread, and this is one of those recipes. This one started from the bottom—I was working on a TV segment for *CTV Your Morning* on biscuits vs. scones, and people loved this bacon and chive biscuit that I came up with so much that I knew I had to make it into a sandwich. I played around with different fillings until I landed here: smoked trout and arugula paired with a classic French dressing called gribiche, which I'm thrilled made it into the book. The sauce combines tanginess from the vinegar and cornichons, saltiness from the capers and anchovies, and richness from the Dijon, olive oil, and eggs. Remember to breathe!

Start by making the biscuits. Preheat the oven to 450°F and line a baking sheet with parchment paper.

In a large mixing bowl, whisk together the flour, baking powder, baking soda, sugar, garlic powder, and salt. Add the cubed cold butter and, using your fingers, cut it into the flour mixture until the mixture is crumbly and the butter pieces are the size of coarse crumbs. Place the bowl in the fridge for 5–10 minutes to rechill the butter.

Remove the bowl from the fridge and mix in 1¼ cups cheddar (reserving ¼ cup to top the biscuits before they go in the oven) plus the bacon and chives, and pour in the chilled buttermilk. Using a fork, gently mix until combined—being careful not to overmix—until it forms a ragged dough.

Turn the dough onto a floured work surface and bring it together to form a ball.

Using your hands, pat the dough into a rectangle. Fold the bottom half of the rectangle onto itself to meet the middle, and then fold the top half over the bottom. Gently pat the dough back into a rectangle, flouring the surface as needed, and repeat the folding process three more times. When patting the dough out the last time, shape it into a 10-inch square about ½ inch thick.

CONTINUED

Using a floured 3-inch round cutter, cut out nine biscuits (do not twist the cookie cutter when cutting, as this will seal the biscuit edges and prevent them from rising beautifully) and place them on the prepared baking sheet. The scraps of dough can be gathered together to make a few more biscuits. If you prefer square biscuits, cut the dough into nine equal pieces. Place the baking sheet in the fridge to chill the biscuits, for about 20 minutes.

Brush the biscuits with buttermilk and sprinkle with the reserved grated cheddar and a tiny bit of flaky salt. Bake for 16–18 minutes or until the tops are nicely browned. Remove from the oven and let cool before making the sandwiches. Store the biscuits in an airtight container at room tempaterure for up to 3 days or in the fridge for up to 1 week.

To make the sauce gribiche, combine both mustards, the olive oil, and the sherry vinegar in a mixing bowl and whisk for about 30 seconds. Fold in the cornichons, capers, anchovies, egg, parsley, and tarragon, and season with pepper.

To assemble the sandwich, split four biscuits in half and spoon a generous amount of sauce gribiche over the bottom of each biscuit. Top with a few slices of trout, a bit of arugula, and then the other half of the biscuit. Your friends and family will most definitely be impressed.

Breakfast Frittata Sandwich

EGGS / CHORIZO / COTIJA / CORN / POTATO / SLOW-ROASTED TOMATO MAYO / FOCACCIA

MAKES 4–6 SANDWICHES

FOCACCIA

5½ cups all-purpose flour

1½ tbsp kosher salt

2¼ tsp active dry yeast (one ¼ oz/8 g packet)

2¾ cups warm water (105°F)

½ cup extra-virgin olive oil

1 tbsp flaky salt

2 sprigs fresh rosemary, chopped

2 sprigs fresh thyme, chopped

SLOW-ROASTED TOMATO MAYO

2 cups cherry tomatoes, halved

2 tbsp extra-virgin olive oil

1 tsp kosher salt

1 tsp cracked black pepper

½ cup mayonnaise

FRITTATA

6 large eggs

¼ cup whole milk

Kosher salt and cracked black pepper

2 chorizo sausages, casings removed

1 tsp extra-virgin olive oil

½ red onion, thinly sliced

6–7 baby potatoes, sliced into ¼-inch rounds

1 ear corn, kernels removed

2 cloves garlic, finely minced

⅓ cup crumbled cotija (if you can't find cotija, substitute with feta)

ASSEMBLY

Roughly chopped fresh flat-leaf parsley and dill for garnish

This sandwich has four elements, and each plays a crucial role—think of it as an orchestra. While an orchestra has its strings, woodwinds, brass, and percussion, this sandwich has its eggs, fillings, mayo, and focaccia; take one away, and it just doesn't work. Can you imagine an orchestra without its violins (some say the most important instrument, but this is a book on sandwiches, not orchestras, so I won't get into that here)? The point being, this sandwich needs a bit more attention than some of its friends in this book, but the results are worth it.

Two of the elements are make-ahead: the focaccia and the slow-roasted tomato mayo. As much as I want you to follow this recipe to a T and make your own focaccia, I understand that time can be a factor. That's why I'll give you a pass and let you buy the focaccia from your favorite bakery. Just promise me that you'll make it eventually—it's a straightforward recipe and, who knows, it could become one of your new go-to's. In fact, this whole sandwich is straightforward; it just needs a bit of planning. And to that point, you can start the dough the night before you plan on serving this, pop it in the fridge, and let it rise while you sleep. All it needs is a bit more attention in the morning and you'll have beautifully fresh focaccia that will have everyone asking for seconds.

One last thing: please don't skip the mayo part of this recipe! The slow-roasted tomatoes become sweet and a bit punchy, and when mixed with the unctuous creamy mayonnaise, they just sing!

We start with the focaccia: I've written this part of the recipe for ease of reading; for ease of working, slow-roast your tomatoes while the focaccia is having its second rise.

Place the flour, salt, and yeast in a large mixing bowl and whisk to combine. Gently pour the warm water into the bowl and, using a wooden spoon or silicone spatula, stir until a very sticky rough dough has formed. Leaving the dough in the bowl, lightly oil your hands and knead the dough for 3–4 minutes.

Add ¼ cup olive oil to a large, clean bowl and use your hands to coat the inside of the bowl with it. Carefully transfer the dough to the oiled bowl, cover it with plastic wrap and let it sit at room temperature for 15 minutes.

CONTINUED

After 15 minutes, stretch and fold the dough by gently taking hold of one side and stretching it out to meet the other side. Give the bowl a quarter turn and repeat this three more times. Cover the bowl with plastic wrap and place it in the fridge for 15 minutes. Repeat three more times, stretching and folding the dough, every 15 minutes (a total of four times over an hour). Cover the bowl with plastic wrap once more and let it chill in the fridge overnight.

The next morning, add 2 tbsp of olive oil to a 13 × 18-inch rimmed baking sheet (or a 9 × 13-inch baking pan for a thicker focaccia) and brush the oil over the bottom and sides to coat. Transfer the dough into the prepared pan, cover the dough with plastic wrap, and place it in a warm spot to rise for about an hour to an hour and a half or until it has filled the pan considerably and the dough has almost reached the edge of the pan. This depends on the temperature of your kitchen (it could take longer, so be patient!)

Preheat the oven to 450°F.

If you're using a 13 × 18-inch baking sheet, do your best to stretch the dough so it fills the pan. If the dough is being finicky and bounces back, cover and let it rest for 5–10 minutes. If you're using a 9 × 13-inch pan, the second rise should have done all the work and filled the pan for you. Use your fingers to poke dimples all over the dough—have fun with this, it can be quite therapeutic! Pour the remaining 2 tbsp of olive oil over the dough, letting it fill all those dimples. Sprinkle with the flaky salt, rosemary, and thyme. Bake for 20–25 minutes if using a 13 × 18-inch baking sheet, or 25–30 minutes if using a 9 × 13-inch baking pan, until nicely browned and the edges are crisp. Remove from the oven and stare lovingly at the focaccia as it sputters and dances with oil on the hot baking sheet. It's my favorite part of this recipe (well, maybe second favorite, because ripping off a piece of warm focaccia straight out of the oven is a gift you will not soon forget! Just make sure you let it cool for 5 minutes before doing that—I don't want to be responsible for you burning yourself!). Once cooled for 5 minutes, transfer to a wire rack to finish cooling.

For the slow-roasted tomato mayo, turn the oven to 400°F and line a baking sheet with foil. In a bowl, toss the tomatoes with the olive oil and season with salt and pepper. Place the tomatoes on the prepared baking sheet and roast for about 40 minutes, or until beautifully blistered and just slightly charred.

Remove from the oven and let cool (leave the oven on, as you will be using it shortly for the frittata). Once cooled, place the roasted tomatoes and all the juices that may have pooled on the baking sheet in a food processor; blend until smooth (you can also use a high-speed blender if you prefer). Transfer the processed tomatoes to a bowl, add the mayo, and mix until nicely combined. If you're like me and can't wait to taste this supercharged mayo, go ahead and rip off a piece of focaccia and dunk it in for an extra-special preview of what's to come—you won't be disappointed.

Onto the frittata: Combine the eggs and milk in a large mixing bowl and whisk until everything is incorporated. Season with salt and pepper and set aside.

Heat a cast-iron pan over medium-high heat. Add the chorizo, breaking it up with a wooden spoon. Cook for about 6–7 minutes or until nicely browned. Using a slotted spoon, remove the chorizo to a bowl and set it aside. If there is a lot of oil left in the pan, omit the olive oil; if the pan is a bit dry, add the olive oil. Add the onion and sauté for 2–3 minutes. Add the potatoes and continue to sauté for an additional 5 minutes. Add the corn and garlic, continue cooking and stirring for another 2–3 minutes, then season with salt and pepper.

Pour the egg mixture into the pan over the potato and corn mixture, then scatter with the cooked chorizo and crumbled cotija. Cook for 2–3 minutes undisturbed. Turn off the heat and place the pan directly into the oven to finish cooking, about 10–15 minutes or until set.

Once out of the oven, let the frittata rest for a few minutes and then slice it into four to six pieces. Cut the focaccia into your desired-sized pieces and then slice them in half crosswise. If you're making this sandwich with focaccia fresh out of the oven, there is no need to toast it. If the focaccia is not fresh out of the oven or if it is store-bought, toast the slices first. Slather a generous amount of tomato mayo onto both sides. Top one side with a slice of frittata and a scattering of chopped herbs, close the sandwich, and enjoy!

NOTE

If you're making focaccia just for the heck of it (and not for a specific sandwich) have fun trying out some different toppings. Try topping your unbaked focaccia with some caramelized onions and cherries from page 85, or a generous sprinkling of za'atar, or some thinly sliced peaches (topped with a drizzle of Salted Caramel Ganache from page 209 when it comes out of the oven). Or try topping a freshly baked focaccia with a generous drizzling of runny honey, a sprinkling of chili flakes, and some orange zest. Or, better yet, create your own personalized focaccia toppings and have fun!

Another Grilled Cheese Sandwich

TALEGGIO / CARAMELIZED ONION / CHERRY / PISTACHIO / SOURDOUGH

MAKES 4 SANDWICHES

CARAMELIZED ONIONS AND CHERRIES

⅓ cup extra-virgin olive oil

3 lb (1.36 kg) (about 3–4 large) yellow onions, halved and thinly sliced

2 tsp kosher salt

2 cups frozen cherries, thawed and well drained

1 tbsp balsamic vinegar

½ tsp cracked black pepper

ASSEMBLY

8 slices sourdough, lightly toasted

8 thick slices Taleggio

⅓ cup pistachios, finely chopped

NOTE

You'll see caramelized onions appear in a few other recipes in this book, and it's a good technique to master. While they do take a bit of time to make, remember what the Persian poet Saadi said "Have patience. All things are difficult before they become easy." Once you get the hang of it, you'll be making them like a pro, I promise you.

If Taleggio is hard to find, replace with Fontina, Gruyère or even Brie, and your sandwich will be equally tasty.

Here we go: another grilled cheese sandwich (to follow my trio on pages 27–28). By the time you get through this book, you'll probably have guessed that any version of grilled cheese is my favorite type of sandwich. I mean, crusty, toasty buttered bread with melted cheese is my kind of heaven indeed. Include some delicious add-ons, like caramelized onions, roasted cherries, and Taleggio—and come on! As with all the sandwiches in this chapter, this one can and should be enjoyed at any time of day, but it's here to prove that you don't need egg or bacon in your sandwich to call it a breakfast sandwich. Here's to grilled cheese sandwiches for breakfast, lunch, and dinner!

We'll start with the caramelized onions. You'll want to use a relatively large stainless-steel pan for this (12 inches works best) so the onions have plenty of room to work their magic. Heat the oil in the pan over medium-high heat. Once the oil begins to glisten, add the onions and salt.

Cook the onions for about 3 minutes without stirring. At this point, they will have begun to soften. Stir the onions well, then let them cook for another 3 minutes undisturbed. Continue doing this until all the onions have developed color, about 20 minutes. Turn the heat down to low and cook for an additional 35–40 minutes, or until the onions have turned a deep brown, occasionally stirring to ensure they don't burn. At this point, the onions will be beautifully caramelized and almost ready. Add the cherries, balsamic vinegar, and the pepper to the pan and stir to combine. Remove from heat.

Preheat the oven to 400°F and line two baking sheets with parchment paper.

To assemble these sweet and savory sandwiches, divide the toast between the two prepared baking sheets. Add the caramelized onion mixture to the toasts on one baking sheet, and two slices of Taleggio to each of the toasts on the other sheet. Place both baking sheets into the hot oven for 2–3 minutes or until the cheese is melted and bubbling. Remove from the oven and sprinkle the cherry and onion sides with chopped pistachios. Sandwich them together and enjoy!

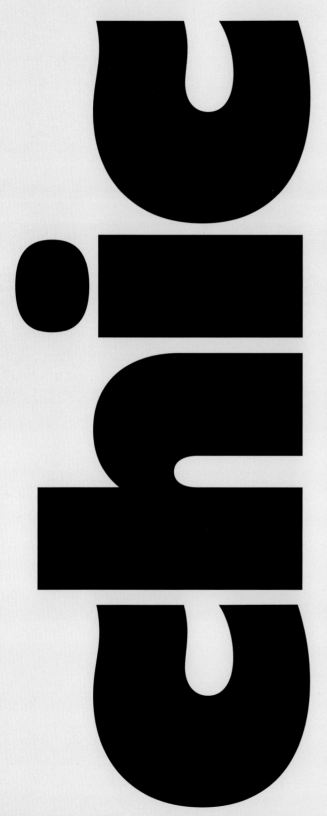

There was a phase in my life, let's say from my late 20s and into my late 30s or even early 40s (is that too long a period to be called a phase?), when all I wore were dress clothes. If you knew me during this part of my life, you know it was dress pants, dress shirts, suit jackets, and fancy dress shoes every day. And I didn't even work in an office! I spent most of that time of my life working the front of house at fancy restaurants in downtown Toronto and running around TV studios working on cooking shows. I've moved on from that and am very happy with my current wardrobe of sweatpants, workout shorts, tank tops, sweatshirts, and sneakers. But every once in a while there is an event, dinner, or wedding, and getting dressed up is necessary. It makes pulling out the fancy clothes I rarely wear fun and exciting. That's what I hope you feel when making the sandwiches in this chapter. Chic sandwiches are not something you would make every day (although you certainly could) but are here to save the day when friends are coming over for dinner and you want to serve them something casual yet still look like you put in a lot of effort.

From a fancy BBQ salmon sandwich with a crown of cucumber ribbons fit for a queen (page 112) to a fried soft-shell crab sandwich with apple slaw and creamy rémoulade (page 117), these sandwiches don't just say hello when they hit the table; they sing it, like Whitney Houston singing "I Wanna Dance with Somebody (Who Loves Me)." Here's hoping a kitchen dance party follows, my sandwich-loving friends! PS: kitchen dance parties are the best, if you don't already know.

STOP HATING EGGPLANT!

FRIED EGGPLANT / SPICED PEANUT SAUCE / PURPLE CABBAGE SLAW / BRIOCHE

MAKES 6 SANDWICHES

PURPLE CABBAGE SLAW

2 cups thinly sliced purple cabbage

2 carrots, shredded

¼ red onion, thinly sliced

⅓ cup roughly chopped fresh cilantro

2 tbsp extra-virgin olive oil

2 tbsp rice wine vinegar

1 tsp toasted sesame oil

1 tsp runny honey

1 tsp kosher salt

1 tsp cracked black pepper

SPICED PEANUT SAUCE

½ cup crunchy or smooth natural peanut butter (only use natural; i.e., no sugar added or try the recipe on page 50)

½-inch knob fresh ginger, finely grated

2 cloves garlic, finely grated

1 tbsp runny honey

1 tbsp soy sauce

1 tbsp rice wine vinegar

1 tbsp chili crisp (if you can't find chili crisp, use 1 tsp chili flakes)

6–7 tbsp warm water (depending on how thin you like your sauce)

EGGPLANT

½ cup cornstarch

1½ tsp kosher salt

1½ tsp cracked black pepper

1½ tsp Kashmiri chili powder

1 tsp ground ginger

2 large eggs

2½ cups panko

1 large or 2 small eggplants, sliced into 1-inch rounds

Neutral oil for frying, such as grapeseed or sunflower

Flaky salt to finish

I hear from people all the time that they "hate" eggplant. It's one of those vegetables that doesn't get much love. Don't get me wrong; I can see why there is such disdain for this nightshade—if cooked improperly, the skin can be mushy, and the taste a bit bitter. But I'm hoping this sandwich might convert a few eggplant haters! I wanted to create a fried eggplant sandwich that would satisfy not only my vegetarian friends but also my carnivore friends. One complaint from carnivores is that vegetarian sandwiches usually lack the oomph that a meaty sandwich can have. I think the double-dredged crispy fried eggplant was a good start, but it needed something else to take it up a notch. Enter my spiced peanut sauce. The combination of peanut butter, ginger, honey, soy, and chili perfectly matches the eggplant. (Make this sauce for the sandwich but keep some in the fridge to drizzle over salads or use as a dipping sauce.) And I top that all off with a simple slaw that rounds out this hefty sandwich. Oh, and don't substitute the brioche bun. It is the perfect partner. I hope you enjoy this as much as I do!

Begin by making the purple cabbage slaw. Combine the cabbage, carrots, red onion, and cilantro in a large mixing bowl and gently toss. In a separate small bowl, whisk to combine the olive oil, vinegar, sesame oil, honey, salt, and pepper. Pour the dressing over the slaw and toss until well coated. Cover and refrigerate until ready to use (coleslaw loves to be chilled so don't skip this step).

Next up is the peanut sauce. As with many sauces in this book, this one's relatively simple to make. In a mixing bowl, whisk to combine all the ingredients except the water. Slowly add a bit of water and continue to whisk until your desired consistency is reached. Add more water if you like your sauce to be a bit runnier.

Prepare your eggplant dredging station by setting out three bowls. In the first bowl, whisk to combine the cornstarch, salt, pepper, chili powder, and ginger. Place the eggs in the second bowl and whisk. Place the panko in the third bowl.

Line a baking sheet with paper towels and place a wire rack on top. In a heavy-bottomed pot, heat about ½ inch of oil over medium heat.

Dredge the eggplant slices first in the cornstarch mixture, then in the egg, and then in the panko—but we're not stopping there. We want the crispiest eggplant for this sandwich, so back into the egg and then one last dunk in the panko! Press the panko firmly but

CONTINUED

89

ASSEMBLY

6 brioche buns

gently into the eggplant to ensure you have a secure coating and most of it stays on while frying.

Gently place a few slices of dredged eggplant into the hot oil and fry for about 4 minutes, flipping halfway through. Remove to the wire rack and sprinkle with flaky salt. Continue frying until all the eggplant slices are fried.

To assemble, spread a generous amount of spiced peanut sauce onto the bottom halves of the buns and top each with a piece or two of fried eggplant. Drizzle with a bit more peanut sauce and top with a nice mound of slaw and the top halves of the buns. Enjoy!

Eggplant Love

I talk about my love of eggplant a few times in this book, but allow me to indulge you on the subject here. Although not as popular as some rivals in the produce section, like tomatoes and potatoes, eggplants are actually from the same family of veggies, the nightshade family—a group of flowering plants that includes everything from the aforementioned veggies to spices like cayenne and paprika to flowers like petunias to shrubs and even weeds. Eggplant—aubergine, as it's called in Europe, or brinjal, as it's known to South Asians—contains 95% water. For this reason, it's great at absorbing flavor and is delicious when roasted or fried.

When thinking about our friend the eggplant in relation to sandwiches, what might come to mind first is the ever-popular fried eggplant parmesan sandwich. Let's be honest, eggplants love a good fry. And there's a reason for this: they're so spongy when raw that they absorb lots of flavors and they can become almost melty when fried. Pair that with a beautifully crispy exterior, and you have the beginnings of a dreamy sandwich.

Here are a few more little-known facts about this extremely lovable nightshade:

- The first recorded mention of eggplant comes from the ancient Chinese agricultural text *Qimin Yaoshu* in 544 CE.
- The name *eggplant* came about because one of its varieties grows white and in the shape of a goose egg.
- As with other members of the nightshade family, trace amounts of nicotine are found in the eggplant's seeds. Don't worry, though, the amount of nicotine in a single eggplant won't show up on your next physical.

If we look at worldwide production and popularity the mighty eggplant sits comfortably at #5 of the most metric tons produced, with approximately 56 million metric tons annually. That's a lot of eggplant! No wonder it's a star in cuisines from China and India to the Middle East. Italy and Greece can't get enough, the French love it, and so do North Americans. Curious what the other top four are? Cabbage and cucumber sit at #4 and #3 with 71 million (that was a surprise to me!), onions come in at #2 with 93 million and, not surprisingly, the belle of the ball, the tomato, comes in at #1 with a whopping 177 million metric tons produced annually around the globe. Wondering how else to use the mighty eggplant? Try sautéing or grilling it!

GILL'S SWEET & SAVORY ONE

HONEY MUSTARD PORK LOIN / ROASTED FIG / PRETZEL BUN

MAKES 8 SANDWICHES

PRETZEL BUNS

1½ cups lukewarm water

1 tbsp maple syrup

2¼ tsp active dry yeast (one ¼ oz/8 g packet)

4¼ cups bread flour

¼ cup unsalted butter, melted

1½ tsp kosher salt

½ cup baking soda

10 cups water

1 large egg, whisked

Coarse salt

DIJON MUSTARD PORK LOIN

2 tbsp extra-virgin olive oil

2 tbsp Dijon mustard

2 tbsp finely chopped fresh rosemary

1 tsp smoked paprika

1 tsp onion powder

1 tsp garlic powder

1 tsp kosher salt

1 tsp cracked black pepper

½ tsp cayenne

3 lb (1.36 kg) boneless pork loin roast

HONEY ROASTED FIGS

2 tbsp apple cider vinegar

2 tbsp runny honey

Zest and juice of 1 orange

6 large or 10 small fresh figs, stems removed and quartered

ASSEMBLY

⅓ cup mayonnaise

1 head Bibb lettuce

A few words about this sandwich: salty, sweet, and savory with a touch of spice. If there were a prize for the most well-rounded sandwich, this one might snag first place. It's also relatively easy to make, but if you decide to make the pretzel buns yourself, there will be a bit more work. I included the pretzel bun recipe because they are not as easy to find as, say, a brioche bun, which has become a grocery store staple these days. By all means, if you don't feel like baking them (and can't find them in a store), substitute a potato bun or brioche bun and you'll be golden.

The night before we shot this sandwich, I felt the recipe needed one last test. Exhausted from the days of shooting we'd been doing, my friend Gill stepped in to help me perfect the recipe. She's a wicked cook, and you can tell from this recipe—thanks, Gillian!

We're going to start with the pretzel buns. Place the warm water, maple syrup, and yeast in the bowl of a stand mixer fitted with the dough hook. Let the yeast sit in the warm maple water for about 4–5 minutes or until the mixture turns frothy.

Add the flour, melted butter, and salt and turn the mixer on to medium speed. Knead the dough for 6 minutes. At this point, the dough will become soft, smooth, and no longer sticky.

Place the dough in a large lightly oiled mixing bowl, turn it a few times to coat it in the oil, and cover it with a damp tea towel. You'll want a slightly warm place for the dough to rise. The dough is ready for the next step when it has doubled in size, about 1–1½ hours.

Line two baking sheets with parchment paper and spray with cooking spray. Do your best to divide the dough into eight equal portions, or better yet, use a scale for perfectly portioned dough, and then form them into balls. Place them on the prepared baking sheets and cover with damp tea towels to let them rise again for about 30 minutes.

Preheat the oven to 450°F and arrange the racks in the bottom and middle sections of the oven.

While the buns are rising, prepare a baking soda bath by adding the baking soda and water to a large pot and bringing it to a boil, mixing well to ensure the baking soda has dissolved. Once the buns have risen for the second time, it's time to give them a bath.

CONTINUED

93

Using a slotted spoon, carefully lower a bun into the water bath and boil for 15 seconds, then flip and boil for another 15 seconds. Remove the bun to a prepared baking sheet, score the top with a slit or an X, whichever you prefer, brush with the whisked egg, and sprinkle with coarse salt. Repeat until all buns have been bathed, scored, brushed, and salted.

Bake both baking sheets of pretzel buns at the same time for 12 minutes. Swap the positions of the baking sheets and bake for an additional 12 minutes. Remove from the oven and let cool on the baking sheets. Turn down the oven temperature to 325°F.

Now let's prepare the pork loin. In a mixing bowl, combine the olive oil, Dijon, rosemary, paprika, onion powder, garlic powder, salt, pepper, and cayenne. Mix well, then rub it all over the pork. Place the pork fat side down in a baking dish and let it sit for 30 minutes so it can rid itself of the chill from the fridge.

Prepare the figs for roasting: In a medium mixing bowl, whisk together the vinegar, honey, orange zest and juice. Add the figs, toss everything together, and place the figs and all that lovely liquid in the baking dish around the pork.

Roast everything for 25 minutes. Baste the pork and return the dish to the oven for another 30–35 minutes. The pork is ready when an instant-read thermometer inserted into the center of the roast reads 145°F. Remove from the oven and transfer the pork to a plate with the figs. Tent with foil to let rest for 10 minutes.

While the pork rests, pour the roasting juices into a small pot and place on the stove over medium-high heat. Bring to a boil, reduce the heat to medium, and let it bubble away until it reduces to become thick and glossy, about 10–12 minutes.

Uncover the pork, slice it, and you're ready to assemble.

To assemble, slice the pretzel buns in half. Slather a generous amount of mayonnaise on both the bottom and top halves of the pretzel buns. Top the bottom halves with a piece of Bibb lettuce, a few slices of pork, some roasted figs, and a drizzle of the reduction. Finish with the top halves of the buns and enjoy! If there happens to be any leftover pork, store it in a container in the fridge for 3–4 days.

THE COVER MODEL

FRIED CHICKEN / (NOT SO) SECRET SAUCE / GREENS / BRIOCHE

MAKES 6 SANDWICHES

FRIED CHICKEN

2 cups buttermilk

¼ cup Buffalo-style hot sauce

¼ cup pickle juice

6 large skin-on, boneless chicken thighs (see note)

2 cups all-purpose flour

⅓ cup cornstarch

1 tsp smoked paprika

1 tsp onion powder

1 tsp garlic powder

1 tsp baking powder

1 tsp kosher salt

1 tsp cracked black pepper

8 cups neutral oil for frying, such as grapeseed or sunflower

Flaky salt

(NOT SO) SECRET SAUCE

½ cup mayonnaise

1 Tbsp ketchup

1 Tbsp grainy mustard

1 Tbsp yellow mustard

1 tsp vinegar-based hot sauce (more for a spicier sauce)

1 tsp runny honey

1 dill pickle, finely minced

½ tsp chili flakes

½ tsp cracked black pepper

GREENS

½ head romaine, shredded

½ bunch lacinato kale, shredded (also known as dinosaur kale, cavolo nero, black kale, or Tuscan kale)

2 tbsp chopped fresh dill

1 tbsp extra-virgin olive oil

1 tbsp pickle juice

½ tsp kosher salt

1 tsp cracked black pepper

I have probably made this sandwich more than any other in this book. It's the one I get requests for the most, and I understand why. Fried chicken sandwiches are overwhelmingly loved. They have an almost king-like stature, so popular in North America that they rival the burger as one of the most loved sandwiches on any menu. Speaking of menus, this was the only sandwich that made it to both my Toronto and UK sandwich-tasting parties. Loved by all who had it, those parties solidified its rightful place on the cover of this book.

The real trick to a super-tender and juicy fried chicken is buttermilk. Buttermilk's gently acidic nature works perfectly to ensure your chicken is moist and tender, and it helps increase the flakiness of the coating. The two other elements of this sandwich, the sauce and the greens, are, in my opinion, perfect partners. The sauce has a touch of sweetness, a touch of tang, and a hint of spice. At the same time, the greens bring in a lively, fresh aspect that rounds everything out. They make such a simple yet delicious salad that I've started to make it as a side dish when serving overly heavy dishes at dinner parties. So there you go, a winning sandwich and a salad topper that you can use as a side at your next shindig. Winner, winner, chicken dinner!

First, let's get the chicken thighs marinating. In a large mixing bowl, whisk together the buttermilk, hot sauce, and pickle juice to create a marinade. Place the chicken in the marinade, cover, and refrigerate for at least an hour or overnight.

You can make the sauce while the chicken marinates, to get ahead of the game. In a mixing bowl, stir together all the ingredients and there you have it, a not-so-secret sauce, done!

Assemble the greens by mixing the romaine, kale, and dill in a bowl. Add the oil, pickle juice, salt, and pepper and toss to coat. Set aside.

It's chicken-dredging time. In a medium bowl, whisk together the flour, cornstarch, paprika, onion powder, garlic powder, baking powder, salt, and pepper.

Line two baking sheets with paper towels and place a wire rack on top of each; you'll use one now and one after the chicken is finished frying.

CONTINUED

ASSEMBLY

6 brioche buns, sliced in half and toasted

Remove the chicken from the fridge and, working with one thigh at a time, transfer from the buttermilk mixture, letting any excess marinade drip back into the bowl, to the flour mixture, ensuring that you have a good solid coating of flour. Place the dredged chicken on one of the wire racks.

Repeat this process until all six thighs are dredged and thoroughly coated in flour. Let the chicken air-dry on the rack for 15 minutes before frying. (Adding fridge-cold chicken to hot oil will reduce the temperature of the oil quickly; bringing the chicken to room temperature will help ensure perfectly crispy fried chicken.)

Add the oil to a Dutch oven and heat to 350°F over medium-high heat. Fry the chicken thighs, two at a time, for about 6–8 minutes, flipping every few minutes to ensure even browning. Once the chicken has reached an internal temperature of 165°F, it is done and can be removed. Place the fried chicken on the clean wire rack to drain any excess oil, and sprinkle with flaky salt. Repeat with the remaining thighs, checking the oil temperature in the Dutch oven and adjusting the heat if necessary to ensure it remains at 350°F.

To assemble, spread about 2 tbsp of (not so) secret sauce on the bottom half of each bun. Top with a piece of fried chicken and a handful of greens. Close the sandwich with the top bun and enjoy!

NOTE

Skin-on, boneless chicken thighs are not the easiest to find. Substituting with skinless, boneless here is just fine. Or see note on page 198 on how to easily debone a chicken thigh.

THE WILD DUCK

DUCK / WILD MUSHROOM / PARMESAN / BAGUETTE

MAKES 4 SANDWICHES

DUCK

2 (14–16 oz/400–454 g) boneless, skin-on Muscovy duck breasts

Kosher salt and cracked black pepper, for seasoning

MUSHROOMS

1 small red onion, thinly sliced

2 cloves garlic, finely minced

1½ lb (680 g) mixed wild mushrooms

1 tbsp Worcestershire sauce

1 tsp cracked black pepper

1 tsp finely chopped fresh thyme leaves

1 tsp finely chopped fresh rosemary

A few handfuls of arugula

ASSEMBLY

1 baguette, sliced into 4, split down the middle, toasted, and buttered

Lots of finely grated parmesan

A wild night out in London was how this sandwich came to be (as you can read about on page 71), and I think you'll agree that late-night sandwiches are almost always the best sandwiches. I say this is a special-occasion sandwich. (Although I probably say somewhere else in the book that every sandwich deserves a special occasion. But I digress . . .) This sandwich is like that time of year when you get to break out your winter clothes. You haven't worn them in a long time, the weather has turned chilly, and there's nothing like the excitement of pulling out your favorite sweater and wrapping yourself in it. That's how I feel when I eat this sandwich.

There is something about cooking a duck breast that I think intimidates most people. It's just not a commonly used protein, so most folks have no idea how to cook it. Well, I'm here to let you know that it's not as hard as you think. Follow the instructions and call me if you have any questions, but I think you'll be fine—I believe in you! I've paired the duck breast with some wild mushrooms and a beautiful dusting of finely grated parmesan. Please wear your favorite sweater when you eat this sandwich, and send me a picture.

Preheat the oven to 400°F and line a baking sheet with parchment paper.

We're going to start by prepping and cooking the duck. Using a sharp knife, trim the breasts of any excess fat and score the skin in a crosshatch pattern, ensuring that you don't cut all the way down to the flesh. Season both sides with salt and pepper.

Place a cast-iron pan on the stove, lay the breasts skin side down in the pan, and turn the heat to medium. You're looking to slowly render the fat underneath the skin without burning it. Let the duck cook undisturbed for 10 minutes, then flip and cook for 2 minutes with the flesh side down. Flip once more so the skin is again kissing the pan. Turn off the heat and place the pan in the hot oven for 5 minutes. Remove the pan from the oven and insert an instant-read thermometer into the thickest part of the breast. You're looking for about 145°F for medium-rare doneness. When it's ready, remove the duck from the pan, place it on a cutting board, and let it rest.

To make the mushrooms, place the pan back on the stove over medium-high heat. Add the onion and cook for 3 minutes, then add the garlic and mushrooms. Sauté for about 5–6 minutes, until the mushrooms have cooked down significantly. Add the Worcestershire sauce, pepper, herbs, and arugula and continue to

cook for an additional 1–2 minutes, until the arugula has wilted nicely. Set aside.

Now that the duck has adequately rested, slice it against the grain (see page 55 for tips).

To assemble, scoop the mushroom mixture onto the bottom slices of toasted and buttered baguette and top with sliced duck breast and lots of grated parmesan. Sandwich with the top slices of baguette and enjoy!

SHRIMP PO'BOY

SHRIMP / HOT HONEY BUTTER / MAYONNAISE / ICEBERG LETTUCE / FRENCH ROLL

MAKES 4 SANDWICHES

SHRIMP

½ cup all-purpose flour

½ cup cornmeal

2 tsp kosher salt

1 tsp garlic powder

1 tsp onion powder

1 tsp smoked paprika

1 tsp cayenne

1 tsp cracked black pepper

1½ cups buttermilk

1 large egg, lightly beaten

2 tbsp hot sauce

1 lb (454 g) large shrimp (21/25 count), peeled, deveined, and tails removed

Neutral oil for frying, such as grapeseed or sunflower

HOT HONEY BUTTER

5 tbsp unsalted butter

2 tbsp runny honey

2 tbsp hot sauce

ASSEMBLY

4 French rolls

⅓ cup mayonnaise

2 cups shredded iceberg lettuce

This recipe makes my mouth water just thinking about it. This is my take on the classic Southern po'boy, with the addition of hot honey butter to satisfy that salty-sweet thing many of us love and crave. The addition of plain, unadulterated tangy mayonnaise and crisp, fresh iceberg lettuce rounds out the flavors in this sandwich. I would never normally suggest that one particular time of year is better than another for any sandwich, but this po'boy sure does scream summer to me. How wonderful would it be if you lived in a cold climate and were presented with a sandwich like this on a frigid day? Take a bite, close your eyes, and escape to a warmer place through the power of a sandwich!

When frying anything, you want to ensure you are completely prepared before you begin. For the shrimp, set yourself up with one unlined baking sheet or larger plate. Line another baking sheet with paper towels and place a wire rack on top.

In a mixing bowl, mix together the flour, cornmeal, salt, garlic powder, onion powder, paprika, cayenne, and black pepper. In a second bowl, whisk together the buttermilk, egg, and hot sauce.

Dunk the shrimp into the buttermilk mixture and then into the flour mixture, then place on the unlined baking sheet or plate. Once all the shrimp are prepped, you're ready to fry.

Fill a large heavy-bottomed pot with 1½ inches of oil and turn the heat to medium. Using an instant-read thermometer, you'll know it's ready when the oil has reached 350°F.

Carefully lower four shrimp into the hot oil and fry, occasionally turning them for even color, for about 4 minutes. Remove the shrimp and place them on the wire rack. Repeat with the remaining shrimp.

Once all the shrimp are fried, it's time to make the hot honey butter. This is simple: place the butter, honey, and hot sauce in a small pot over medium heat and stir constantly until everything is combined.

It's assembly time! Transfer the fried shrimp to a large mixing bowl. Set aside ¼ cup of the hot honey butter and pour the rest over the shrimp. Toss until the shrimp are well coated.

Cut open the rolls and spread liberally with mayonnaise. Nestle in some shredded lettuce and top with some shrimp. Because the hot honey butter will have absorbed into the shrimp a bit, drizzle with a bit more just before serving. Enjoy!

(BUT IT IS A PULLED LAMB SANDWICH)

SURPRISE, NOT ANOTHER PULLED PORK SANDWICH

PULLED LAMB / PRESERVED LEMON / YOGURT / FRISÉE / BAGUETTE

MAKES 8–10 SANDWICHES

LAMB

2½ lb (1.1 kg) boneless lamb shoulder

Kosher salt

½ cup extra-virgin olive oil

2 yellow onions, chopped

2 carrots, chopped

3–4 cloves garlic

1 tsp ground cumin

1 tsp smoked paprika

1½ cups passata

½ cup runny honey

2 cups chicken stock

Peel of half an orange

3 sprigs each fresh rosemary, thyme, and mint

1 tbsp unsalted butter

¼ cup Quick Preserved Lemons (see recipe on page 104), minced or ½ preserved lemon, rinsed and minced

YOGURT SAUCE

½ cup Greek yogurt

Zest of ½ lemon

1 tsp runny honey

½ tsp cracked black pepper

ASSEMBLY

2 baguettes, each sliced into 4–5 pieces each, split down the middle, and toasted

⅓ cup niçoise olives, pitted and halved

1 head frisée, torn

Who needs another pulled pork sandwich? Not me, that's for sure. But I do love the slow-cooked and tender meat that pulled pork delivers. So, I thought, why not do the same with lamb? The process is the same, except we're using lamb shoulder instead of pork shoulder. Like its porky cousin, lamb shoulder is quite affordable (compared to other cuts of lamb) and when braised becomes juicy and full of flavor. If you're new to braising, at its core it's simply slow-cooking something in liquid at a low temperature.

Preheat the oven to 325°F. Use a paper towel to pat the lamb dry and season liberally on all sides with kosher salt.

Heat ¼ cup of the olive oil in a Dutch oven or heavy-bottomed pot over medium-high heat. Sear the lamb on all sides for about 4–5 minutes, until nicely browned and a beautiful crust has formed. Remove the lamb to a plate and gingerly pour off the fat.

Add the remaining ¼ cup of olive oil along with the onions, carrots, and garlic to the Dutch oven and cook, stirring occasionally, for about 5 minutes. Add the cumin and paprika and stir to coat the veggies. Add the passata, honey and chicken stock, stir well and bring to a boil. Remove from the heat and nestle the lamb shoulder back in the Dutch oven. Surround the lamb with the orange peel and fresh herbs, cover, and place in the oven to braise for 3 hours.

Remove from the oven and let the meat rest with the lid on for 30 minutes. Once it's rested, place the lamb in a large bowl and strain the braising liquid, discarding the vegetables, herbs and orange peel. Return the braising liquid to the Dutch oven, skim off any fat, and bring it to a boil over medium-high heat. Let the liquid reduce for about 10–12 minutes or until it coats the back of a spoon. Add the butter, whisk to combine, and remove from the heat. The sauce is now ready to wrap itself around the lamb and give it a giant hug.

Using two forks, shred the lamb into bite-sized pieces. Pour ¼–½ cup of the sauce, depending on how saucy you like your sandwiches, over the lamb and mix to combine. Fold in the preserved lemons.

To make the yogurt sauce, place all the ingredients in a bowl and mix to combine.

To assemble, spread a liberal amount of yogurt sauce on the bottom slices of baguette and gently nestle in a generous amount of the lamb mixture. Top with a few olives and a bit of frisée. Close the sandwiches with the top slices of baguette and enjoy.

Quick Preserved Lemons

Let's talk about the wonderfully bright, delicately tart, and extraordinarily lemony preserved lemons. I love how they complement this sandwich, and how you can add them to salads, stews, or soups, or toss them with roasted vegetables or in a batch of lemon cupcakes.

4 lemons (preferably organic), scrubbed with warm water to wash off any wax

2 tbsp granulated sugar

2 tbsp kosher salt

2 tbsp extra-virgin olive oil

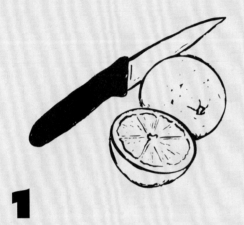

1

Roughly chop the lemons and discard the seeds.

2

Add the lemons to a large mason jar, ensuring that as much lemon juice as possible is included.

3

Add the sugar, salt, and oil and mix well. Cover and let sit at room temperature for 24 hours.

4

Give the jar a good shake every so often to give the lemon pieces a chance to mingle. These preserved lemons will keep, covered in the fridge, for up to 2½ weeks.

ANOTHER SANDWICH FOR DAD

VEAL SCHNITZEL / ARTICHOKE /
LEMON TARRAGON BROWN BUTTER MAYO / CAPERS / PARSLEY / KAISER

MAKES 4 SANDWICHES

LEMON TARRAGON BROWN BUTTER MAYO

¾ cup unsalted butter, cubed

1 large egg yolk

1 tsp Dijon mustard

Juice of ½ lemon

½ tsp kosher salt

1 tbsp roughly chopped fresh tarragon

VEAL

1½ lb (680 g) veal cutlets (about 8 slices)

3 tbsp Dijon mustard

Kosher salt and cracked black pepper

½ cup all-purpose flour

1½ cups dried breadcrumbs

⅓ cup finely grated parmesan

3 large eggs

¼ cup heavy cream

Neutral oil for frying, such as grapeseed or sunflower

ASSEMBLY

4 kaiser rolls, sliced in half and toasted

12 jarred artichokes, patted dry and halved

2 tbsp capers

1 cup fresh flat-leaf parsley leaves

My parents' influence on my cooking is all over this book, including in this recipe. Being an immigrant from Slovenia, my dad's cooking reflected his upbringing. Most Eastern European countries have a version of schnitzel, and Slovenia is no different. But since my mom did most of the cooking while I was growing up, we didn't eat much meat. After my mom had my twin brother and me, she embraced a low-key vegetarian lifestyle for our family, cooking a lot of vegetarian casseroles that would await us upon our arrival from school every afternoon.

Some weekends my dad would take over cooking duties, and schnitzel was one thing he would often make. I remember being very young and always wanting to help in the kitchen. My dad would prop me up on a stool so my short arms and little hands could reach the counter and help him dredge the veal (or chicken or pork). We would inevitably make a mess, but I think he enjoyed the "help." If there were ever any leftover dredging ingredients, we would make little pancakes out of them and fry them up in the dirty oil. Memories of being in the kitchen with my dad are special to me, and I think he would have loved this sandwich.

For the mayo, melt the butter in a medium sauté pan over medium heat. Swirl the pan frequently to prevent the butter from burning. Cook until it browns and smells nutty, about 5–7 minutes. Remove the pan from the heat and immediately transfer the butter to a small mixing bowl to let cool completely.

Place the egg yolk, Dijon, lemon juice, and ¼ tsp salt in a blender. Blend on high for 20–30 seconds and then slowly drizzle in the cooled brown butter; you'll want to drizzle it in very slowly to ensure a lovely creamy consistency. When ready, transfer the mayo to a bowl and gently fold in the tarragon. Taste and adjust the seasoning as needed.

Pat the veal cutlets dry with paper towels and lay them on a cutting board. If the veal is not already pounded, place cutlets between two pieces of plastic wrap and pound with a meat mallet until they are about ¼ to ⅛ inch thick. Lightly spread the Dijon onto both sides of each cutlet and liberally season with salt and pepper.

CONTINUED

105

Prepare the dredging station, using two plates and a bowl. Place the flour on one plate. On the second plate, mix to combine the breadcrumbs and parmesan. In the bowl, whisk together the eggs and cream.

Dredge a veal cutlet in the flour, then dip into the egg mixture, letting any excess drip off. Finally, place the veal in the breadcrumb mixture and press it in to ensure the whole cutlet is coated. Place on a clean plate until ready to fry. Repeat with the remaining cutlets.

Line a baking sheet with paper towels and place a wire rack on top. In a large skillet, heat about ½ inch of oil over medium heat. Working in batches of two or three cutlets at a time, fry one side of the cutlets for about 3 minutes, then flip and fry the other side for 3 minutes more. Remove to the wire rack and sprinkle with a bit more salt. Repeat until all the cutlets are done.

To assemble, spread the mayo onto the bottom half of each kaiser roll and top with veal schnitzel and some artichokes. Sprinkle with capers and parsley, close with the bun top, and enjoy!

LOBSTER ROLL

LOBSTER / ANCHOVY MAYO / PANINI ROLL

MAKES 6 SANDWICHES

ANCHOVY MAYO

¾ cup mayonnaise

2 tsp grainy mustard

3 anchovy fillets, finely chopped

2 green onions, thinly sliced

1 clove garlic, finely grated

2 tbsp minced fresh chives

1 tsp cracked black pepper

½ tsp smoked paprika

Zest of 1 lemon

ASSEMBLY

1½ lb (680 g) cooked lobster meat (fresh or frozen and thawed), patted dry and chopped into bite-sized pieces

6 Italian panini rolls, sliced, toasted, and buttered

Minced chives for garnish

Short on time but need something to impress your guests for your next summer backyard party? This is the sandwich for you. I don't expect everyone to know how to cook and prepare a lobster, so do the next best thing: buy it frozen. No shame in that at all.

The anchovy mayonnaise comes together quickly, and it's such a great addition to this sandwich. The sweet lobster meat and the salty anchovy mayo go on a first date and, let me tell you, this relationship lasts!

To make the anchovy mayo, place everything in a bowl and mix to combine.

To assemble, mix the lobster meat and anchovy mayo in a large bowl, then divide among the toasted, buttered buns. Garnish with chives and enjoy!

MORGAIN'S SAUCEBOX

SPICY CHICKPEAS / VEGGIES / TURMERIC TAHINI MAYO / MULTIGRAIN

MAKES 4 SANDWICHES

VEGGIES

1 eggplant, sliced into ½-inch rounds

1 bulb fennel, cored and thinly sliced

1 medium zucchini, sliced into ¼-inch rounds

1 medium red onion, sliced into rounds

2 red bell peppers, seeded and cut into strips

2 tbsp extra-virgin olive oil

1 tsp kosher salt

1 tsp cracked black pepper

TURMERIC TAHINI MAYO

½ cup mayonnaise

¼ cup tahini

1 tbsp maple syrup

Juice of ½ lemon

1 clove garlic, finely grated

½ tsp ground turmeric

½ tsp curry powder

¼ tsp kosher salt

CHICKPEAS

1 (28 fl oz/796 mL) can chickpeas, drained and well rinsed

2 tbsp extra-virgin olive oil

½ tsp smoked paprika

½ tsp chili flakes

½ tsp ground cumin

½ tsp kosher salt

ASSEMBLY

8 slices multigrain bread, toasted

8 pieces leaf lettuce

Veggie lovers tend to get the short end of the stick when it comes to sandwiches. I say this from experience, as my friend Morgain recently asked me, "Jason, can you make me a veggie sandwich that doesn't suck?" Challenge accepted, my friend! Chickpeas feature prominently in many veggie sandwiches, but I wanted to jazz things up with this one. A bit of spice, a few minutes in a hot pan, and a bit of smashing, and these chickpeas are transformed into the perfect fit for a sandwich. Pair this with some beautifully charred veggies and we're almost there.

The final key to this sandwich is the sauce (let's be honest, it's always the sauce). The combination of creamy mayonnaise, nutty tahini, and peppery turmeric brings everything together—slather on a bit extra; I won't tell anyone! Speaking of sauce, Morgain loves sauce, so it's fitting that I named this saucy sandwich after her; in fact, we all call her Saucebox for her love of sauce and her saucy vibe (she's going to hate me for telling you that). We also call each other Mary, but that's a long story; feel free to ask me if we happen to be in a long line together and need to kill some time.

Preheat the oven to 450°F and line two baking sheets with parchment paper.

Arrange the veggies on the prepared baking sheets, drizzle with olive oil, and season with salt and pepper. Roast for 25–30 minutes, or longer if you like things a bit charred. Remove from the oven and set aside.

While the veggies are roasting, make the turmeric tahini mayo: combine everything in a mixing bowl and whisk until smooth. As this mayo is quite thick, feel free to loosen it a bit with a few teaspoons of water if you like your sauce a bit thinner. Set aside.

Time for the spicy chickpeas. In a mixing bowl, combine the chickpeas, olive oil, paprika, chili flakes, cumin, and salt. Mix well to coat the chickpeas. Transfer everything to a pan over medium-high heat and cook for about 7–8 minutes, stirring frequently. Remove from the heat and slightly mash the chickpeas with a fork or a potato masher.

To assemble the sandwiches, liberally spread the turmeric tahini mayo on four slices of the toasted bread. Top each slice with lettuce, some roasted veggies, and a scoop of spiced chickpeas, then close the sandwich with the other slice of toast. Enjoy!

THE PRETTY ONE

BBQ SALMON / PANCETTA / CUCUMBER / LEMON GARLIC AIOLI / CIABATTA

MAKES 4 SANDWICHES

CITRUS BBQ SAUCE

1½ cups ketchup

Zest and juice of 1 lime

Zest and juice of 1 orange

¼ cup dark molasses

3 tbsp apple cider vinegar

1 tbsp sriracha (optional)

1 tbsp Worcestershire sauce

1 tbsp Dijon mustard

1 tsp smoked paprika

1 tsp onion powder

1 tsp kosher salt

½ tsp garlic powder

¼ tsp liquid smoke (optional)

LEMON GARLIC AIOLI

2 large egg yolks, at room temperature

3 cloves garlic, finely grated

1½ tsp Dijon mustard

Juice of ½ lemon

½ cup extra-virgin olive oil

½ tsp kosher salt

SALMON

4 (4–6 oz/115–170 g) skin-on salmon fillets

3 tbsp extra-virgin olive oil

1 tsp kosher salt

1 tsp cracked black pepper

ASSEMBLY

4 ciabatta buns, sliced in half and toasted

8–12 slices pancetta, crisped

1 cucumber, shaved into thin ribbons

She's pretty, isn't she? Not all sandwiches can say they wear a billowing crown of cucumber ribbons, but this one sure can! A lot is going on here; some may be tempted to say too much, but trust me, dear readers, every part of her is meant to be there. The tangy citrus BBQ sauce that the salmon has been encased in kisses the aioli, and let me tell you, if you're a fan of saucy sandwiches, this one will have you singing! Not to mention the crunch and salt from the pancetta and the freshness of the cucumber. I just decided this sandwich might win best in show!

Like some of the other sauces in the book, you'll have some leftover BBQ sauce after you make this sandwich. But that's okay; store it in a mason jar in the fridge for up to 3 weeks and use it on everything from wings to burgers and even homemade pizza. The aioli is another one of those recipes-within-a-recipe. It's wonderful with this sandwich but can be used in so many other ways, like on your favorite sandwich or even as a dressing for roasted vegetables. It's like your favorite three-for-one sale, but in a recipe (is three-for-one a thing?).

Let's begin by making the BBQ sauce. In a medium pot over medium heat, combine the ketchup, lime and orange juices (not the zest quite yet!), molasses, vinegar, sriracha (if using), Worcestershire, Dijon, paprika, onion powder, salt, garlic powder, and liquid smoke (if using). Mix well and bring to a boil. Reduce the heat to low and let the sauce simmer for about 20–25 minutes. Remove from heat and stir in the lime and orange zest. Set aside.

Next up is the aioli. Place the egg yolks, garlic, Dijon, and lemon juice in a large mason jar or the container of your immersion blender. To make the aioli, you need to emulsify it. Emulsifying is taking two liquids that do not usually mix—in this case, the oil and the egg yolks (yolks are 50% water)—and turning them into a semi-stable mixture. Slowly drizzle in the olive oil and use your immersion blender to blend, moving it up and down until the aioli has thickened. Add the lemon juice, blend for a few seconds more to combine and season with salt and set aside.

Now it's time for the salmon. Crispy skin is what we're looking for here. Pat the salmon fillets with a paper towel, ensuring all sides are nice and dry. Rub a bit of oil on both sides and season with salt and pepper. Heat the remaining oil in a nonstick skillet over medium-high heat. Once the oil in the pan begins to shimmer, place two salmon fillets skin side down in the pan, pressing them down firmly, and cook undisturbed for about 4 minutes; you want to make sure that the skin is crispy and releases from the pan easily.

Carefully flip the salmon fillets so they are skin side up. Slather the skin and sides with the citrus BBQ sauce and cook an additional 2–3 minutes. Flip once more so the salmon skin is again kissing the pan, and slather the other side with a generous amount of BBQ sauce. Cook for 30 seconds more. Remove the salmon from the pan and repeat with the two remaining fillets. Let the cooked salmon rest for a few minutes before assembling the sandwich.

To assemble, spread a generous amount of lemon aioli on each of the top and bottom halves of each bun. Layer the sandwich by placing a salmon fillet on the bottom bun, followed by two or three slices of crispy pancetta, some cucumber ribbons, and the top bun. Enjoy!

THE PRETTY HAPPY DREW

GRILLED HALLOUMI / BEET / POTATO CHIPS / RUSSIAN DRESSING / BRIOCHE

MAKES 4 SANDWICHES

POTATO CHIPS

1 lb (454 g) russet potatoes, thinly sliced lengthwise (⅛ inch is ideal)

Neutral oil for frying, such as grapeseed or sunflower

1 tsp kosher salt

HALLOUMI

1 tbsp extra-virgin olive oil

4 (1 inch thick) slabs of halloumi (approximately 3 inches square)

ASSEMBLY

4 brioche buns, toasted and buttered

1 recipe Russian Dressing (page 240)

1 large beet, peeled, grated, and squeezed until dry

NOTE

If you're not into making the chips yourself, buy your favorite brand; the sandwich will be just as tasty as if you made them yourself.

"I think happiness is what makes you pretty. Period. Happy people are beautiful. They become like a mirror, and they reflect that happiness." —Drew Barrymore

I agree, Drew, and I also think you can substitute "people" with "sandwiches" and it's still a pretty damn good quote. This is a happy sandwich, and it will make *you* happy when you make it and eat it. I also think it's a pretty sandwich, sitting all tall and confident with its soft, buttery brioche bun, crispy and slightly salty potato chips, sweet dark magenta grated beets, and golden fried halloumi. And the dressing brings it all together and helps it shine even more. I think Drew would approve, don't you?

You'll start this sandwich by making the chips—and feel free to make extra; I guarantee you no one will object! (Or skip this step and use a bag of your favorite chips.) Place the potato slices in a large bowl and fill the bowl with cold water. Let the slices sit in the water for 10 minutes, swishing them around every few minutes to release the starch, and then drain. Repeat this process one more time, then place the potato slices on paper towels and pat dry.

Line a baking sheet with paper towels and place a wire rack on top. Fill a heavy-bottomed pot with about 4 inches of oil and place over medium-high heat. Heat the oil to 350°F, then gently add about a third of the potato slices. Fry the potatoes, flipping them every 10–15 seconds with a slotted spoon or metal spider. Continue to fry until nicely golden on both sides, about 8–10 minutes. Remove the chips from the oil to the wire rack and sprinkle with salt. Repeat until all the potato slices have matured into chips. Set aside, but promise me you'll eat a few along the way.

The halloumi needs to be eaten right after frying, so start your assembly now. Slather the bottom halves of the buns with Russian dressing to have them ready to go.

To fry the halloumi, heat the oil in a cast-iron pan over high heat. Add the halloumi to the hot oil and fry for about 2–3 minutes per side; you want to see some nice browning on each side.

Assemble the sandwiches—time is of the essence here! Place a slice of fried halloumi on the bottom half of each bun, add some grated beet, top with potato chips, and close with the top bun. Enjoy!

SOFT-SHELL CRAB SANDWICH

RÉMOULADE / APPLE / BACON / BRIOCHE

MAKES 4 SANDWICHES

RÉMOULADE

½ cup mayonnaise

¼ cup cornichons, finely diced

2 tbsp capers

1 tsp Dijon mustard

1 tsp grainy mustard

1 tsp finely chopped fresh dill

1 tsp finely chopped fresh flat-leaf parsley

Juice of 1 lemon

SLAW

1 Honeycrisp apple, cored and julienned

½ small red onion, thinly sliced

1 tbsp finely chopped fresh chives

1 tbsp finely chopped fresh dill

6 slices bacon, cooked until crisp and roughly chopped

2 tbsp extra-virgin olive oil

Juice of 1 lemon

¼ tsp kosher salt

½ tsp cracked black pepper

SOFT-SHELL CRAB

1 cup all-purpose flour

½ cup cornmeal

2 tsp Old Bay seasoning

2 large eggs

1½ cups panko

Neutral oil for frying, such as grapeseed or sunflower

4 soft-shell crabs, cleaned and patted dry (get your fishmonger to clean the crabs, as this is not something you will want to tackle once you bring the crabs home, trust me!)

ASSEMBLY

4 brioche buns, toasted

Soft-shell crab is available fresh for only a short window of time each year (generally, where I live in Canada, that is late spring to early summer). If you can find it fresh, grab some and make this sandwich. If you happen to miss the season, use frozen.

The sauce we are using for this sandwich is a French sauce called rémoulade. It has similarities to the English tartar sauce, and some may say to Thousand Island or Russian dressing. It always starts with mayonnaise, and I've used Dijon and a host of other ingredients to round it all out. Anything fried, like the soft-shell crab here, loves to be paired with something creamy, so be liberal with the sauce and slather on a bit more than you might think it needs. To finish the sandwich, we add a fresh and tart apple slaw. I guarantee that this sandwich will make an impression on your guests.

Let's start by making the sauce and the slaw. For the rémoulade, place all the ingredients in a bowl and mix well to combine. Refrigerate until needed.

For the slaw, in a bowl, mix the apple, onion, chives, dill, and bacon. Drizzle with the olive oil and lemon juice, and season with salt and pepper. Toss to coat, cover and refrigerate until needed.

For the crab, set out your dredging station with three medium bowls. In the first, mix together the flour, cornmeal, and Old Bay. Crack the eggs into the second bowl, and beat. Place the panko in the third bowl.

Line a baking sheet with paper towels and set a wire rack on top. Heat about 3 inches of oil in a large heavy-bottomed pot set over medium-high heat. The oil will be ready to fry when a wooden skewer inserted into it starts to bubble around the edges.

Dredge the crabs first in the flour and cornmeal mixture, then in the egg, and finally in the panko, pressing the breadcrumbs onto the crab to ensure maximum coverage.

Gently lower two crabs at a time into the hot oil and fry for about 3 minutes. Flip and fry on the other side for 3 more minutes. Remove from the oil and place the fried crabs on the wire rack. Repeat with the two remaining crabs.

To assemble the sandwiches, spread a generous amount of rémoulade onto both the bottom and top halves of the buns. Place a fried soft-shell crab onto each sauced bottom half, top with a handful of slaw, and finish with the top bun. Enjoy!

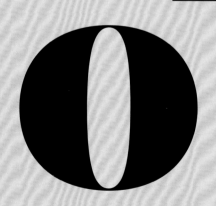

OPEN

No offense, open-faced sandwich, but you were a last-minute addition to this party, and you almost didn't make it. I was conflicted because I wasn't convinced that an open-faced sandwich was indeed a sandwich and deserving of a place, let alone a whole chapter, in this book. But after much thought and counsel, I decided to give you a chance. And I'm sure glad I did, because you sandwiches are natural beauties. You've got a different vibe than the rest of the sandwiches in the book—a bit of a rebel, throwing caution to the wind by ditching the top and letting it all hang out.

Anchovies, eggplants, pumpkin seed oil, roasted garlic, and toasted coconut are just some of the influential players you associate yourself with in this chapter. I'm getting ready to take my taste buds for a ride!

Lamb! Eggplant! Breadcrumbs! Feta!

LAMB / BABA GHANOUSH / HERBY BREADCRUMBS / FETA / SOURDOUGH

MAKES 4 SANDWICHES

LAMB

1 tbsp unsalted butter

1 tbsp extra-virgin olive oil

1 small yellow onion, diced

2 cloves garlic, finely grated

½ tsp ground cumin

½ tsp chili flakes

¼ tsp cayenne

¼ tsp kosher salt

½ tsp cracked black pepper

½ cup passata

⅓ cup kalamata olives, chopped

1 lb (454 g) ground lamb

BREADCRUMBS

2 tbsp extra-virgin olive oil

1 cup panko

1 tsp kosher salt

⅓ cup finely chopped fresh flat-leaf parsley and mint

Zest of ½ lemon

ASSEMBLY

1 recipe Baba Ghanoush (page 51)

4 slices thick-cut sourdough, toasted

1 cup crumbled feta

I know I'll be asked repeatedly what my favorite sandwich in this book is, and the answer will always be the same: there is no way I can pick a fave. But I can pick a few standouts: those sandwiches that I go back to repeatedly and never get tired of eating—and this is one of them.

For this sandwich I've paired baba ghanoush with a simple, thick lamb sauce, some herby breadcrumbs for a nice crunch, and some salty feta to round everything out. It's plated on some toasty sourdough, and I tell you, this sandwich is like having a party in your mouth. Honestly, you might even want to start dancing. And if you do, may I recommend something from Madonna's seventh studio album, *Ray of Light*. It's futuristic electronica meets trip-hop with traces of Eastern influences and even a bit of drum and bass. Something for everyone, just like this sandwich. Enjoy, friends!

Let's start with the lamb. Heat the butter and oil in a Dutch oven or large pot over medium-high heat. Add the onion and sauté until softened, about 6–7 minutes. Add the garlic and continue to sauté for another minute. Season with the cumin, chili flakes, cayenne, salt, and pepper, then add the passata and olives. Mix to combine and let everything become friendly for a few minutes. Add the ground lamb and break it up with a wooden spoon. Continue to cook until the lamb has browned, about 7 minutes. Turn the heat down to low and let the mixture simmer for about 15 minutes, until most of the liquid evaporates and the mixture has thickened. Turn the heat off and set the lamb aside.

For the breadcrumbs, heat the olive oil in a medium pan over medium-high heat. Add the panko and fry, stirring frequently to prevent burning, for about 3–4 minutes. Stir in the salt and herbs and fry the breadcrumbs for another 1–2 minutes. Remove from heat and mix in the lemon zest. Set aside.

To assemble, smear a generous amount of the baba ghanoush onto each slice of toasted sourdough and top with a few heaping spoonfuls of lamb. Finish with a sprinkling of breadcrumbs and feta. Enjoy!

NOTE You'll find the baba ghanoush for this recipe in the Fresh Falafel recipe (page 51). Feel free to keep it on hand for use in other sandwiches you feel inspired to create.

(THE "OH MY, I THINK I'M IN LOVE" SANDWICH)

Steak Tartare on Toast

STEAK / YOLK / PUMPKIN SEED OIL / PUMPERNICKEL

MAKES 4 SANDWICHES

TARTARE

1 lb (454 g) beef tenderloin

¼ cup finely chopped cornichons

3 tbsp capers, drained and finely chopped

3 tbsp finely chopped fresh flat-leaf parsley

1 tbsp finely chopped red onion

2 tbsp pumpkin seed oil

1 tbsp Dijon mustard

¼ tsp kosher salt

½ tsp cracked black pepper

ASSEMBLY

4 pieces pumpernickel, toasted

4 large egg yolks

Flaky salt

I love steak tartare. There's a restaurant in London's Soho district called Café Boheme that my friend Morgain and I always have lunch at, especially in the summer, when we sit on their sidewalk patio and watch as all the characters of Soho walk by. It's excellent people-watching if you're ever in London. We only ever order one thing when we're there: steak tartare. Well, two things, as we always wash it down with a glass or two of Ruinart Blanc de Blancs, Brut NV.

Whenever I have steak tartare, whether at Café Boheme or some-place else, I always order more toast. You cannot eat steak tartare without toast, so why not make it an open-faced sandwich?

The addition of the pumpkin seed oil in this recipe is a nod to my father. He always had pumpkin seed oil in the kitchen and would use it mainly as a salad dressing, but the earthiness lends itself well to the richness of the steak and the creaminess of the egg yolk. If pumpkin seed oil is challenging to find, drizzle on some extra-virgin olive oil.

To start, make the tartare. Finely chop the beef and add to a medium mixing bowl (see note). Add the cornichons, capers, parsley, onion, pumpkin seed oil, Dijon, salt, and pepper and gently mix until thoroughly combined.

To assemble, divide the tartare between the pieces of toasted pum-pernickel, top each with an egg yolk, and garnish with a drizzle more pumpkin seed oil and some flaky salt. Enjoy!

NOTE

If you find it hard to finely chop the beef, place it in a food processor and let the machine do all the work. Pulse a few times and you'll be golden.

That Sandwich I Ate When I Was in My 20s

TART APPLE / WHITE CHEDDAR / HONEY MUSTARD / MARBLE RYE

MAKES 4 SANDWICHES

HONEY MUSTARD SAUCE

3 tbsp grainy mustard

3 tbsp mayonnaise

2 tbsp Dijon mustard

1 tbsp runny honey

½ tsp cracked black pepper

ASSEMBLY

4 slices marble rye

2 Granny Smith apples, cored and thinly sliced

1½ cups shredded white cheddar

Zest of 1 lemon

There was a restaurant in Toronto's Kensington Market called the Bellevue Diner that I worked at in my early 20s. If you don't know Kensington, it's a busy place with fruit markets, butchers, bakeries, fishmongers, cheese shops, and bars and restaurants. The weekends are hectic, with restaurant lineups for Saturday and Sunday brunch service, let me tell you!. If you knew me in my 20s, you might remember that I enjoyed late nights on the dance floor and perhaps a few too many gin and tonics. This did not make for a very enjoyable Sunday brunch service.

The kitchen staff, my friend Morgain (whom I met while working there), and I would all arrive at the same time to get the restaurant ready for the impending crowds. We knew they were coming, and it was the last place we wanted to be, so we needed sustenance. We would put on a fresh pot of coffee, and the aroma that filled the air gave us a sense of hope that service would be okay. We would squeeze cases of fresh oranges to fill countless jugs and all the while, the kitchen would be blaring *Rumors* by Fleetwood Mac and making us breakfast. Our go-to order was multigrain bread, thin slices of tart Granny Smith apple, and white cheddar grilled cheese sandwiches. While it may not have made the crowds more amicable, it did help with the hangover.

This sandwich is a nod to that grilled cheese we ate weekend after weekend and never got bored with. I've updated it, made it an open-faced sandwich, and added a creamy honey mustard sauce. I hope you enjoy it as much as we enjoyed its long-lost cousin.

To make the honey mustard, place all the ingredients in a small bowl and whisk to combine. Cover and refrigerate until needed.

Preheat the oven to 450°F and line a baking sheet with parchment paper.

Place the marble rye slices on the prepared baking sheet and into the oven for 2–3 minutes. Flip and toast the other sides for an additional 2–3 minutes. Remove the baking sheet from the oven and spread the mustard sauce onto one side of each slice of toast. Cover with apple slices and sprinkle with cheddar cheese. Return to the oven for 2–3 minutes or until the cheese has fully melted and is bubbly. Sprinkle with lemon zest and enjoy!

Mortadella for Life!

ROAST CHERRY TOMATO / STRACCIATELLA / MORTADELLA / FOCACCIA

MAKES 4 SANDWICHES

ROAST CHERRY TOMATOES

3 cups cherry tomatoes

4 sprigs fresh rosemary

¼ cup extra-virgin olive oil

1 tsp kosher salt

1 tsp cracked black pepper

ASSEMBLY

1 recipe focaccia (page 81)

7 oz (200 g) mortadella

5 oz (140 g) stracciatella

Fresh basil for garnish

Extra-virgin olive oil to drizzle

Flaky salt for garnish

The focaccia in this recipe can be found on page 81 and can also be used in a few other sandwiches in this book. If you've never made focaccia, I suggest you try it. But if you're busy with life and everything it can throw at you, feel free to buy a loaf and call it a day. And if you've decided to forgo making your own focaccia, this recipe will come together fairly quickly and is perfect for a lazy Sunday brunch.

Let's quickly talk about stracciatella. In Italian culinary terms, *stracciatella* can refer to three things: an ancient Roman soup, a creamy gelato studded with dark chocolate from the Lombardy region, or what we are using today, a cheese from the southeastern region of Puglia. This soft cheese is really just the inside of burrata, which also hails from Puglia. *Stracciatella* means "little rags" and is made by mixing leftover pieces of mozzarella with fresh cream. If you're having a hard time finding it but can get your hands on some burrata, tear into that and let all of its beautiful insides pour out. And if burrata is hard to find, get your hands on some fresh mozzarella, tear it up, and use it instead. This sweet, creamy, and sumptuous cheese is a perfect pairing with the smoky roast tomatoes and the salty, fatty mortadella (you can read more about my love of mortadella on page 186). The basil rounds out the sandwich with its clean, earthy flavors.

Preheat the oven to 375°F.

Make the tomatoes: Place the cherry tomatoes and rosemary in a cast-iron pan and toss with olive oil, salt, and pepper. Roast for 40 minutes. Remove from the oven and let cool.

To assemble, slice the focaccia into two 3-inch squares and then in half. You'll have leftover focaccia, but that's okay because you can store it in an airtight container for 2–3 days (it may need to be heated up or toasted once it's a day old though)—or go ahead and make the Breakfast Frittata Sandwich on page 81 tomorrow!

Mound the four pieces of focaccia with some mortadella, top with a generous amount of stracciatella and some roasted tomatoes, and finish with basil, olive oil, and flaky salt.

The Simple Things

FRESH RADISH / ANCHOVY BUTTER / CHIVE / PUMPERNICKEL

MAKES 4 SANDWICHES

ANCHOVY BUTTER

½ cup unsalted butter, softened

2 cloves garlic, finely grated

4–6 anchovy fillets, finely minced

½ tsp curry powder

½ tsp chili flakes

Zest and juice of ½ lemon

ASSEMBLY

4 slices pumpernickel

6–8 radishes, trimmed and thinly sliced

Handful of fresh chives, chopped

Flaky salt

If there were an award for the most straightforward sandwich in the book, this one might take the prize. It's simple yet powerful and quite elegant; the fresh, crisp, and slightly peppery radish plays oh so nicely with the cool old-timey anchovy butter. It reminds me of that time when Lady Gaga and Tony Bennett teamed up for an album; if they were a sandwich, this would be it. Maybe I should compare each of the sandwiches in the book to celebrities? Or maybe not. Just this one.

To make the anchovy butter, place the softened butter, garlic, anchovies, curry powder, chili flakes, and lemon zest and juice in a medium bowl and mix until well combined. Set aside until needed. Extra butter can be stored in an airtight container in the fridge for up to a month.

To assemble, spread a generous amount of butter onto each slice of bread. Top with lots of radish slices, some chopped chives, and a tiny sprinkling of flaky salt. Enjoy!

129

It's Another Grilled Cheese (Sort Of)

BROCCOLI / FENNEL / ROMESCO / EMMENTAL / MULTIGRAIN

MAKES 4 SANDWICHES

BROCCOLI & FENNEL

1 head broccoli, cut into florets

1 bulb fennel, stalks and fronds removed, cored, and sliced lengthwise into ½-inch pieces

2 tbsp extra-virgin olive oil

2 cloves garlic, finely grated

1 tsp kosher salt

1 tsp cracked black pepper

½ cup finely grated parmesan

KALE ROMESCO

3 jarred whole roasted red peppers (about 7 oz/200 g)

½ cup slivered almonds

¼ cup tomato paste

4 leaves of lacinato kale (also known as dinosaur kale, cavolo nero, black kale, or Tuscan kale), stems removed and roughly chopped

2 cloves garlic, roughly chopped

2 tbsp sherry vinegar

1 tsp smoked paprika

1 tsp kosher salt

½ tsp cracked black pepper

¼ cup extra-virgin olive oil

ASSEMBLY

4 slices multigrain bread, toasted

8 slices Emmental

If you've already cooked your way through the Classics chapter (or at least flipped through it), you'll know there are three grilled cheese sandwiches in it. As I said in that intro, I'm a fan of melted cheese between grilled and buttered (or mayo'ed!) bread with other things stuffed into it. Grilled cheese sandwiches excite me, and I don't think I'm the only one.

I created this one because my love of broccoli and fennel knows no bounds. I wanted a grilled cheese that almost felt summery. And while the veggies are roasted before they are added to the sandwich, they retain a slight crunch. Combine that with my romesco sauce with kale, and we're on our way to summer sandwich heaven. Romesco originates in the Catalonia region of Spain and typically includes tomatoes, peppers, nuts (such as almonds, hazelnuts, or pine nuts), garlic, olive oil, and vinegar. Some versions use day-old bread or breadcrumbs to bind the sauce, while others add herbs to flavor it. My version adds kale, a favorite ingredient not only in this book but also in my kitchen. I think you will enjoy it.

First, let's roast those veggies. Preheat the oven to 425°F and line a baking sheet with parchment paper.

Place the broccoli and fennel on the baking sheet, ensuring they are spaced out and not lying on top of each other. In a small mixing bowl, whisk to combine the olive oil, garlic, salt, and pepper. Pour this mixture over the veggies and use your hands to make sure everything is well coated. Roast for 20 minutes. Remove from the oven and sprinkle with parmesan, then continue roasting for another 15 minutes. Remove from the oven and set aside.

Next up is the super-simple romesco sauce. Place the red peppers, almonds, tomato paste, kale, garlic, sherry vinegar, paprika, salt, and pepper in a food processor and pulse a few times to get things going. With the motor running, slowly add the olive oil and continue to process until the sauce has come together.

Turn the oven to broil and line a baking sheet with foil.

To assemble, slather a lavish amount of the sauce on each slice of toasted multigrain. Pile a generous amount of the roasted veggies on top and then finish with the cheese.

Pop the sandwiches onto the foil-lined baking sheet and into the oven for 1 minute, or until the cheese bubbles and melts. Remove from the oven and enjoy!

For Carm

ROASTED PURPLE GRAPE / WHIPPED GOAT CHEESE / PISTACHIO / MINT / SOURDOUGH

MAKES 4 SANDWICHES

ROASTED PURPLE GRAPES

1 or 2 large cluster purple grapes, stems removed

2 tbsp sherry vinegar

1 tbsp extra-virgin olive oil

1 tsp kosher salt

WHIPPED GOAT CHEESE

11 oz (310 g) goat cheese, room temperature

2 tbsp runny honey

1 tbsp extra-virgin olive oil

Zest of ½ orange

½ tsp cracked black pepper

ASSEMBLY

4 slices sourdough, toasted

½ cup pistachios, roughly chopped

¼ cup roughly chopped fresh mint

I remember when I was a kid, my family and I would visit my godmother Carm's place in Toronto all the time. From the moment I was born Carm and I shared an unbreakable bond and her influence on me is reflected in the person I am today. To say that she played an enormous part in my life would be an understatement. She was the person who first introduced me to the fantastical world of cookbooks, and I know that if she were here today this would be the only cookbook on her shelf. Carm, I miss you every day.

Carm's entire backyard was covered in Concord grape vines. Every summer we would make the trek up, and one of the jobs my twin brother and I had was to help her harvest the grapes. The owners of the house before Carm had planted them to make wine, but she was certainly not interested in that. Concord grape jam or jelly is nice, but you need only so much of it in your life. So what did she do with the extra grapes? She roasted them and ate them on toast, a sort of shortcut to jam, you might say.

I've taken this idea and added to it. Here the roasted grapes sit on a pillowy bed of whipped goat cheese and sweet honey, and a crowd of pistachio pieces and fresh mint are balanced on top.

Finish with a wispy drizzling of olive oil, and she's ready for her close-up. I think Carm would approve.

Preheat the oven to 425°F and line a baking sheet with foil.

First, let's roast the grapes. Place them on the prepared baking sheet, toss with vinegar and oil, and season with salt. Roast the grapes for 15–20 minutes or until they have blistered and shrunk in size. Remove from the oven and set aside.

To make the whipped goat cheese, combine the goat cheese, honey, olive oil, orange zest, and pepper in a bowl and mix well, until fully incorporated and smooth.

To assemble, spread or pipe (if you want to be fancy!) the whipped goat cheese onto the toasted sourdough, then top with some roasted grapes, a scattering of pistachios and mint, and a bit of the drippings from the roasted grapes. Enjoy!

A Shocking Hit! A Surprise Standout!

WHITE ANCHOVY / JAMMY EGG / PARSLEY / BAGUETTE

MAKES 4 SANDWICHES

JAMMY EGGS
4 large eggs

ASSEMBLY
1 baguette, sliced into two 5-inch pieces, split down the middle, and toasted

¼ cup unsalted butter, softened

12–20 white anchovies (see note)

2 tbsp roughly chopped fresh flat-leaf parsley

Flaky salt

Cracked black pepper

Aleppo pepper

You know those headlines when a new Broadway show seemingly comes out of nowhere and takes the critics by storm? I'm thinking of *Come from Away*, *Kinky Boots*, or *Avenue Q*. No? Well, for the Broadway novices out there, these shows had no hype going into their opening weekend but made the critics awfully giddy. That's how I feel about this sandwich.

We're revisiting the anchovy with this sandwich, but not the one you might be familiar with. Not the one I've already talked about on page 54. And not the one you think of when you think of pizza. No, sandwich lovers, I'm not talking about the oil-packed anchovies that come in little jars. I'm talking about the glorious white anchovy. The overlooked white anchovy is a secret that I can't keep anymore. Pairing it with jammy eggs, butter, and fresh herbs is like when director Spike Jonze cast Cameron Diaz in *Being John Malkovich*: unexpected, but somehow it worked!

And one thing you should know about me: I have a thing for jammy eggs; I'm not going to lie. My dad used to make them for us growing up, and I'm pretty sure that's where I developed my soft-boiled-egg obsession. Just-set whites and a creamy, runny yolk are perfect to me. Eat it all by itself, dip your toast in there, or cut it open and add it to a salad. Or better yet, make this sandwich and fall in love with the white anchovy too!

We'll start with the jammy eggs. Bring a large pot of water to a gentle boil over medium-high heat and carefully lower in your eggs. Let them hang out in the boiling water, adjusting the heat to maintain a gentle boil, for 6 minutes. Remove the eggs from the pot and immediately place them in an ice bath to cool. (If you are really not a fan of soft-boiled eggs but still want to try this sandwich, go ahead and let the eggs hang out in the pot for a bit longer: 8 minutes for medium-boiled and a whopping 12 minutes for hard-boiled. Play around a bit with timing to suit your taste.)

Once the eggs have cooled, peel them and cut them in half.

To assemble, slather the toasted baguette with butter and place two egg halves on each slice. Divide the anchovies between the sandwiches and sprinkle with chopped parsley. Finish with some flaky salt, cracked black pepper and Aleppo pepper, and enjoy!

NOTE

I've given quite a range in the anchovy amount because I like lots on mine, but feel free to be a little more conservative if you're new to anchovies.

Chelsie Is a Badass, and So Is This Sandwich

WILD MUSHROOM / ROASTED GARLIC / HERB OIL / COMTÉ / SOURDOUGH

MAKES 4 SANDWICHES

ROASTED GARLIC

1 head garlic

1 tbsp extra-virgin olive oil

½ tsp kosher salt

½ tsp cracked black pepper

MUSHROOMS

3 tbsp unsalted butter

1 small red onion, thinly sliced

2 shallots, minced

Kosher salt and cracked black pepper

6 cups mixed wild mushrooms, sliced

1 tsp dried oregano

HERB OIL

2 cups packed fresh basil leaves

2 cups packed fresh flat-leaf parsley leaves

1 cup extra-virgin olive oil

ASSEMBLY

4 slices sourdough, toasted and buttered

½ cup shredded Comté (see note)

It's hard not to love mushrooms, and cooking your way through this book, you'll see them pop up in a few sandwiches. I'm a big fan, and if you're one of the many people trying to eat a bit less meat, mushrooms will be at the top of your go-to list. I've paired them here with some roasted garlic (another favorite in this book) and a killer herb oil. The herb oil is super simple to make and can be used with lots of other things: on eggs (we love eggs), pasta (we love pasta), or soups (we love soup), or, heck, as the base of your very own signature vinaigrette! There will be lots of leftover herb oil, but it stores well in the fridge for a few months.

I named this sandwich after my dear friend and workout partner Chelsie. She's a badass, and so is this sandwich. She packs a punch—the sandwich, not Chelsie, although she does push me in the gym like no one else (thanks, partner!). This sandwich is layered, complex, and richly rewarding, just like a workout with Chelsie.

Preheat the oven to 350°F.

For the roasted garlic, cut the top off the head of garlic and place the bulb on a piece of foil. Coat the garlic with the olive oil and season with salt and pepper. Wrap it tightly into a package and place it on a baking sheet. Roast for 40 minutes. Remove from the oven and set aside.

For the mushrooms, melt the butter in a large skillet over medium heat. Add the onion and shallots, season with salt and pepper, and sauté for 5 minutes. Add the mushrooms and continue to sauté for 6–7 minutes. Remove from the heat, toss with the dried oregano, and adjust the seasoning if needed. Set aside.

For the herb oil, you'll want to have an ice bath on standby. Bring a pot of salted water to a boil. Add the basil and parsley and blanch the herbs for about 15–20 seconds. Immediately remove and transfer them into the ice bath to cool. Once cooled, give them a good squeeze to release as much water as possible, then pat them dry. If you have a salad spinner this would be a good time to use it! The herbs will be very wet, and it's important to make sure they are super dry before moving on to the next step. Once dry, place them in a blender along with the oil. Blitz on high until smooth. Set a fine-mesh sieve over a large mixing bowl and line it with either a coffee filter or some cheesecloth. Pour the mixture into the lined

CONTINUED

137

sieve to drain the oil of all the leftover bits. Once fully drained, transfer to a jar and store it in the fridge until ready to use. This oil will keep in the fridge for a few months.

Turn the oven to broil and line a baking sheet with parchment.

To assemble the sandwiches, unwrap the roasted garlic, squeeze all the soft, sweet cloves into a bowl, and give them a good mashing. Spread the roasted garlic onto each slice of toasted sourdough. Divide the mushrooms between the slices and top each with some shredded Comté. Place under the broiler until the cheese is melted and bubbly. Remove from the oven, drizzle with some of the herb oil, and enjoy!

NOTE If Comté is difficult to find, replace it with Gruyère, Gouda or Cheddar; they'll all work nicely as well.

Squash to the Rescue

ACORN SQUASH / COCONUT GREMOLATA / CURRY MAYO / FOCACCIA

MAKES 4 SANDWICHES

SQUASH

¼ cup unsalted butter, melted

2 tbsp dark brown sugar

1 tsp curry powder

½ tsp ground cinnamon

¼ tsp ground cloves

½ tsp kosher salt

½ tsp cracked black pepper

1 large or 2 small acorn squash, halved, seeded, and sliced into thin rounds

COCONUT GREMOLATA

½ cup unsweetened shredded coconut

½ cup unsweetened coconut chips

¼ cup chopped fresh flat-leaf parsley

¼ cup chopped fresh cilantro

2 tbsp chopped fresh mint

Zest of ½ lemon

½ tsp chili flakes

1 tsp kosher salt

CURRY MAYO

½ cup mayonnaise

Juice of ½ lemon

1 clove garlic, finely grated

½ tsp ground turmeric

½ tsp curry powder

¼ tsp kosher salt

ASSEMBLY

1 focaccia (store-bought or try the recipe on page 81), cut into 2 decent-sized pieces, halved

2 tbsp extra-virgin olive oil

Many people I know are moving away from eating meat daily to a more plant-based diet. I was conscious of this when coming up with recipes for this book, and this recipe proves that plant-based sandwiches can be just as satisfying as their meaty cousins.

I love squash, particularly the varieties with thinner skins that can be roasted whole without peeling. It makes for less prep time and less cleanup—sorry, butternut squash, but you can be a handful! Roasting acorn squash with warm and aromatic spices like curry, cinnamon, and cloves gives the already flavorful squash that extra kick you want. The gremolata in this recipe adds a freshness to the dish while also bringing in some much-needed texture with the coconut.

Mirroring the flavors of the roasted squash with the curry mayo brings it all together. This curry mayo can play a part in other sandwiches too—I'm thinking burgers in particular. Veggie burgers, of course!

Preheat the oven to 400°F and line a baking sheet with parchment paper.

We'll start with the squash. In a large mixing bowl, combine the melted butter, brown sugar, curry powder, cinnamon, cloves, salt, and pepper. Add the squash and toss well, ensuring everything is nicely coated.

Place the squash on the prepared baking sheet drizzle with any remaining butter mixture from in the bowl, and roast for 20–25 minutes. Remove from the oven and set aside to cool. Do not get rid of the parchment-lined baking sheet; you'll use it shortly to toast the focaccia.

While the squash is baking, make the coconut gremolata and the curry mayo. For the gremolata, place the shredded coconut in a small pan over medium-high heat and toast, stirring occasionally. Remove from the heat and transfer to a mixing bowl. Add the coconut chips, herbs, lemon zest, chili flakes, and salt and mix until well combined. Set aside.

For the curry mayo, place all the ingredients in a bowl and mix until well combined. Set aside.

To assemble, place all four pieces of focaccia on the used baking sheet. Drizzle with olive oil and place in the preheated oven for 5 minutes or until nicely toasted.

Smear a generous amount of curry mayo onto each slice of toasted focaccia, followed by a few pieces of squash. Top with a generous sprinkling of coconut gremolata and enjoy!

BUR
GER

Possibly my favorite chapter in this book, although I think I may have said that about every other chapter at some point as well. This chapter had a few naysayers from the beginning, folks who didn't think that burgers deserved or needed to be included in a book on sandwiches. I clearly disagreed. If a burger is not a sandwich, then what is it? Get ready to get your burger game on, because I'm about to take you on a ride! In this chapter are beef burgers, pork burgers, a chicken burger, a turkey burger, a fish burger, a lamb burger, and a veggie burger (yes, sadly, only one veggie burger; I'll do better next time, my veggie friends, I promise!). With toppings such as candied jalapeños, white BBQ sauce, spinach-mint pesto, and red onion and bacon jam, there's something for everyone. And don't forget to have fun using this chapter's toppings and sauces in your own sandwich creations. Happy burger-ing!

INTERNAL TEMPERATURES FOR BURGERS

It's a good idea to have an instant-read thermometer in your kitchen if you cook a lot of meat (it's also useful for baking as well).

Beef burgers:

medium-rare
130°F–135°F

medium
140°F–145°F

medium-well
150°F–155°F

well done
160°F–165°F

Halibut burgers:
130°F–135°F

Lamb burgers:
160°F

Pork burgers:
160°F

Turkey burgers:
165°F

Chicken burgers:
165°F

The Dude

BEEF SMASHED PATTY / CARAMELIZED ONION / AMERICAN CHEESE /
SMOKY & SPICY MAYO / HAMBURGER BUN

MAKES 4 BURGERS

CARAMELIZED ONIONS

1 recipe Caramelized Onions and Cherries (page 85), omit the cherries

SMOKY & SPICY MAYO

½ cup mayonnaise

2–3 chipotles in adobo (depending on your preferred spice level), very finely minced

Zest of 1 lime

1 tsp Dijon mustard

½ tsp cracked black pepper

BEEF PATTIES

1 lb (454 g) ground beef

Kosher salt

2 tbsp extra-virgin olive oil

4 slices American cheese

ASSEMBLY

4 hamburger buns, sliced in half and toasted

NOTE

Wondering what to do with that lonely jar of leftover chipotle peppers in your fridge? There are lots of options! You can chop them up and add them to your next burger patty. Or add them to some homemade salsa or hot sauce for a extra smoky kick. Or blitz them up and add to your next Caesar or Bloody Mary. Or they're wonderful when added to eggs. The possibilities are endless, my friends!

I'm pretty sure that if you're a fan of burgers, you'll be a fan of these smash burgers. They have all the classic trappings you could ask for: smashed patties, caramelized onions, American cheese, and spicy mayo. They're so good that the book's photographer, Séb, took a bite out of one of the burgers we were shooting when I wasn't looking. He later finished all four, so if you're curious about how they taste, I would say reach out to him for a review.

Why is this burger named The Dude? Simple: I couldn't have a burger chapter and not pay tribute to the ultimate burger king, my dear friend Keelan, or the one I call Dude—one of my dearest friends and the one person I know who will always have burgers ready at the drop of a hat. Trust me, show up at his place unannounced and burgers will appear on the grill within minutes. And that's a very good thing, dude.

Start by making the caramelized onions on page 85 (and don't forget to omit the cherries).

To make the smoky & spicy mayo, place all the ingredients in a small bowl and mix to combine. Set aside.

For the burgers, divide the ground beef into four equal pieces and form them into balls. Place the beef balls on a cutting board, cover with parchment paper or plastic wrap, and, using the bottom of a pan, smash them into lovely flat patties. Season both sides of the patties generously with salt.

Heat half the oil in a cast-iron pan over medium-high heat. Add the patties, two at a time, and cook for 3–4 minutes on one side; flip and continue to cook for another minute. Place the cheese slices on top of the burgers, cover, and continue cooking until the cheese is melted.

To assemble, spread a generous amount of the mayo on the four bottom halves of the buns. Top with a cheesy smash burger and a few tablespoons of onions. Finish with the top halves of the buns and enjoy!

A Burger for Spring

PORK PATTY / ASPARAGUS & FETA SLAW / POTATO BUN

MAKES 4 BURGERS

ASPARAGUS & FETA SLAW

6–7 stalks asparagus, shaved into ribbons

1½ cups shredded purple cabbage

⅓ cup crumbled feta

2–3 green onions, thinly sliced

2 tbsp extra-virgin olive oil

1 tbsp apple cider vinegar

1 tsp granulated sugar

½ tsp cracked black pepper

Dash of hot sauce (optional)

PORK PATTIES

1 tsp extra-virgin olive oil

⅓ bunch curly kale, stems removed, finely chopped

1½ lb (680 g) ground pork

2 tbsp full-fat Greek yogurt

Zest and juice of 1 lemon

1½ tsp kosher salt

1 tsp cracked black pepper

½ tsp sweet paprika

1 large egg, beaten

⅓ cup dried breadcrumbs

2 tbsp extra-virgin olive oil

ASSEMBLY

⅓ cup mayonnaise

4 potato buns

Bibb lettuce

Spring on a plate, that's how I would describe this burger. The fresh asparagus and feta slaw pairs well with the pork, and the whole thing comes together quite quickly.

Most people think of asparagus as a vegetable that needs to be cooked, but both times it's used in this book, it's in its raw form. Here we use a vegetable peeler to shave beautiful long ribbons and pair them with crunchy purple cabbage and salty, crumbly feta. Side note: this slaw is lovely on its own and would be delicious as a side with any meal that needs a fresh salad.

To prepare the slaw, toss the asparagus, cabbage, feta, and green onions in a large bowl. In a small bowl, combine the olive oil, apple cider vinegar, sugar, pepper, and hot sauce (if using) and whisk until well combined. Add the dressing to the slaw and toss. Cover and refrigerate until ready to use.

For the burgers, add the 1 tsp oil to a large skillet over medium heat and sauté the kale for 2–3 minutes or until nicely wilted. Remove from the heat and let cool. Place the kale and all the other burger ingredients, except the 2 tbsp oil, in a large bowl and mix with your hands until well combined (do not overmix, as it will make for tough burgers; count to 10 while mixing and you should be good!). Form into four equal-sized patties.

Heat the 2 tbsp oil in a large cast-iron pan over medium-high heat. Add two patties at a time to the pan and cook until the undersides have browned and developed a nice crust, about 4 minutes. Flip the burgers and allow the other sides to do the same. The burgers are done when an instant-read thermometer registers 160°F.

To assemble, slather a bit of mayo on the bottom and top halves of the buns. To the bottom halves, add some lettuce, a patty, and a handful of the slaw. Finish with the top half of the bun and enjoy!

Messy, Eh?

BEEF PATTY / MAPLE BACON / CANADIAN CHEDDAR / WHITE BBQ SAUCE / BRIOCHE

MAKES 4 BURGERS

MAPLE BACON

8 thick-cut bacon slices

¼ cup maple syrup

1 tsp Worcestershire sauce

1 tsp vinegar-based hot sauce

1 tsp cracked black pepper

WHITE BBQ SAUCE

½ cup mayonnaise

1 tbsp prepared horseradish

1 tbsp grainy mustard

1 tsp apple cider vinegar

1 tsp maple syrup

½ tsp Worcestershire sauce

1 tsp cracked black pepper

½ tsp garlic powder

½ tsp onion powder

A few dashes of vinegar-based hot sauce

BEEF PATTIES

1½ lb (680 g) ground beef

Kosher salt

2 tbsp extra-virgin olive oil

4 slices Canadian cheddar

ASSEMBLY

4 brioche buns, sliced in half and toasted

When doing some research a while back on the history of BBQ sauces, I came across something I had never heard of—white BBQ sauce, or Alabama white sauce. It sounded gimmicky to me, but I was intrigued. It turns out a gentleman named Robert Lee Gibson, better known as Big Bob Gibson, of Big Bob Gibson Bar-B-Q invented the sauce nearly 100 years ago in Alabama. As with most things, it was soon copied, and now there are hundreds of versions, including this one you're about to make. Here I pair my white BBQ sauce with some very Canadian maple bacon (easy to make and very easy to eat!) and Canadian cheddar cheese (if you're not from Canada, use whatever cheddar is in your fridge). Messy, yes. But as I've said many times, messy is a good thing when it comes to sandwiches.

We'll start this one with the bacon. Preheat the oven to 400°F, line a baking sheet with parchment and place a wire rack on top. Place the bacon on the wire rack; it's okay if some of the slices overlap, as they will shrink as they cook.

In a bowl, whisk together the maple syrup, Worcestershire sauce, hot sauce, and pepper and brush over both sides of the bacon. Place the bacon in the oven and bake for 18–20 minutes or until the desired crispiness is achieved. Remove from the oven and brush the bacon with any remaining maple syrup. Let cool on the rack.

To make the BBQ sauce, place all the ingredients in a mixing bowl and whisk to combine. Cover and refrigerate until needed.

Divide the ground beef into four equal portions and shape them into patties. Season generously with salt.

Heat half the oil in a cast-iron pan over medium-high heat. Cook two patties on one side for about 5–6 minutes, flip, and place a slice of cheese on the cooked side. Cover, lower the heat to medium-low, and cook until the cheese melts, about 2 minutes. Remove the patties from the pan, add the remaining oil, and repeat with the remaining patties. I've included a handy internal temperature chart for varying doneness at the beginning of this chapter (page 144); use it to help gauge when your burgers are done the way you want them.

To assemble this glorious burger, slather a generous amount of the sauce onto the bottom buns, then top with a cheesy patty and some maple bacon. Close with the top half of the bun and enjoy!

Surf & Turf Burgers

BEEF PATTY / SHRIMP / MANCHEGO / BACON / SWEET & TANGY MAYO / BRIOCHE

MAKES 4 BURGERS

SWEET & TANGY MAYO

½ cup mayonnaise

1 tbsp grainy mustard

1 tbsp yellow mustard

1 tsp maple syrup

½ tsp sweet paprika

Zest of 1 lime

SHRIMP

12 large shrimp, shelled, deveined, and tails removed

1 tbsp extra-virgin olive oil

2 cloves garlic, finely minced

Juice of 1 lime

1 tsp Montreal steak spice (or your favorite steak spice)

1 tsp smoked paprika

BEEF PATTIES

1½ lb (680 g) ground beef

2 cloves garlic, finely grated

1 tbsp finely chopped fresh flat-leaf parsley

1½ tsp Montreal steak spice (or your favorite steak spice)

2 tbsp extra-virgin olive oil

1 cup shredded manchego

ASSEMBLY

4 brioche buns, sliced in half and toasted

4–8 pieces green leaf lettuce

8 slices bacon, crisped

"Surf and turf" typically (but not always) refers to the pairing of filet mignon and lobster, but we're pairing beef burgers with shrimp here—and adding manchego and bacon for the hell of it. Throwing it back to the US in the 1960s, "surf and turf" (that hedonistic and, some might say, slightly kitschy menu item) gained popularity in restaurants on both coasts for its showy presentation and delightfully unexpected partnership. While it may not be as popular on menus as it was in its heyday, I'm pretty thrilled my burger version of "surf and turf" made it into this book, and even more excited for you to try it.

We'll start by making the easiest part of this recipe—the mayo. In a mixing bowl, whisk to combine all the ingredients. Cover and refrigerate until needed.

Next up is the shrimp. Place the shrimp in a large bowl and toss with the olive oil, garlic, lime juice, steak spice, and paprika. Heat a medium skillet over medium-high heat. Add the shrimp and sauté until they have turned pink and the tail ends have curled up, about 2–3 minutes per side. Remove from the pan and set aside. Wipe the pan clean, as you'll use it to cook the burgers.

To make the burgers, place the ground beef, garlic, parsley, and steak spice in a bowl. Use your hands to mix, but do not overmix, as it will make for tough burgers; count to 10 while mixing and you should be good (or sing, "Don't cry. / Don't raise your eye. / It's only teenage wasteland" from The Who's "Baba O'Riley"—I know you know it!). Divide the mixture into four equal portions and shape them into patties.

Heat half the oil in the pan over medium-high heat. Cook two burgers at a time for about 3 minutes on one side, then flip and cook for another 3 minutes on the other. Flip again and divide the shredded cheese among the burgers. Cover the pan and let the cheese melt, about 2 minutes. (Check out the internal temperature guide at the beginning of the chapter, on page 144). Remove the burgers from the pan and you're ready to assemble. Add the remaining oil to the pan and repeat with the remaining patties.

To assemble, spread a generous amount of the mayo onto the bottom halves of the toasted buns. Add one or two pieces of lettuce to each and top with the cheesy patty. Place two pieces of bacon and three sautéed shrimp on top and drizzle with more mayo if you're feeling it. Sandwich with the top halves of the buns and enjoy!

The "My Twin Stopped Eating Meat, So I Came Up with This Burger" Burger

PORTOBELLO / SPINACH-MINT PESTO / TOMATO / MANCHEGO / BRIOCHE

MAKES 4 BURGERS

SPINACH-MINT PESTO

3 cups packed baby spinach

1 cup packed fresh mint leaves

½ cup roughly chopped almonds

2 cloves garlic, roughly chopped

Juice of 1 lemon

⅓ cup extra-virgin olive oil

1 cup finely grated manchego

1 tsp cracked black pepper

PORTOBELLO MUSHROOMS

4 large portobello mushrooms, cleaned, stemmed, and gills removed

⅓ cup extra-virgin olive oil

1 tsp kosher salt

1 tsp cracked black pepper

4 slices manchego

ASSEMBLY

4 brioche buns, sliced in half and toasted

4 tbsp mayonnaise

4 thick slices tomato

1 cup sprouts (use your favorite—I like peppery sprouts such as mustard or radish)

I've been known to say this about many of my sandwiches, but (ugh) I love this one so much! I developed this burger because my twin brother, Ryan, recently moved to a meat-free diet and I wanted something I could make for him when he and my sister-in-law, Afsah, came over for dinner. The challenge was to create a veggie burger that was more about the veggies and less about trying to replicate a meat burger. I tested this burger at their place one night and my brother loved it so much that he took the leftovers with him camping the next day. I say that's a win for this burger.

Portobellos just make sense for a burger, as they are meaty and big and take well to a hot pan. Tomatoes also make sense; I mean, a thick, juicy tomato slice propping up a grilled portobello is perfect. But I think the real hero here is the spinach-mint pesto. It's something you can most certainly take from this recipe and use in other applications, like on fish or chicken or in a salad. If the portobello, tomato, and pesto are like the stars of the show, the melted manchego, sprouts, and mayo are the background players; they're vital for everything to work, allowing the stars to shine.

Begin by making the pesto. Place the spinach, mint, almonds, garlic, and lemon juice in a food processor. Pulse a few times until the mixture has broken down a bit. With the motor running, slowly pour in the olive oil. Continue to process until smooth. Transfer the pesto to a mixing bowl, then fold in the manchego and season with pepper. Cover and refrigerate until needed.

For the portobello mushrooms, brush both sides of the mushrooms with equal amounts of oil and season with salt and pepper. Heat a large skillet over medium-high heat. Place the mushrooms, bottom side down, in the skillet and sauté for about 5 minutes. Flip the mushrooms so the tops are facing down, and brush with any remaining oil. Sauté for another 5 minutes. Flip once more so the tops face up again, and add a slice of cheese. Cover and let the cheese melt.

To assemble, spread a generous amount of the pesto onto the bottom halves of the buns and 1 tbsp mayonnaise to each of the top halves. Top the pesto-covered bottom halves with a tomato slice, a portobello mushroom, and some sprouts. Finish with the top bun and enjoy!

The Allium Burger

CHICKEN PATTY / ASIAGO / CRISPY LEEK / POTATO BUN

MAKES 4 BURGERS

CRISPY LEEKS

Neutral oil for frying, such as grapeseed or sunflower

1 leek, white and pale green parts only, cut into 2-inch-long matchsticks, rinsed, and dried thoroughly

Kosher salt

CHICKEN PATTIES

1½ lb (680 g) ground chicken

¼ cup mayonnaise

¼ cup dried breadcrumbs

3 cloves garlic, finely grated

4 green onions, finely chopped

2 tbsp finely chopped fresh chives

2 tbsp finely chopped fresh flat-leaf parsley

½ tsp chili flakes

½ tsp kosher salt

½ tsp cracked black pepper

4 slices Asiago

ASSEMBLY

⅓ cup mayonnaise

4 potato buns, sliced in half and toasted

1–2 tomatoes, sliced

Chicken burgers. What can I say? They may not be the first thing that comes to mind when thinking of burgers, but they deserve their time to shine. And here, they do shine!

Allium, per the burger's name, refers to the group or genus of flowering plants that includes onions, garlic, chives, leeks, and shallots, among others. I've given this burger a sort of overdose of allium—and I love it. Green onions (or scallions, as they are also known), leeks, chives, and garlic all make an appearance. The crispy leeks add a bit of crunch and a mild but welcome onion flavor. They're straightforward to make and can be used in other things too, like salads, and even to finish a soup. In my humble opinion, a chicken burger needs a bit of melted cheese, and I've chosen Asiago here for its sharp, nutty, creamy flavor. With a bit of added freshness from the tomato, this sandwich is ready for action.

Line a baking sheet with paper towels.

To make the crispy leeks, add about 1 inch of oil to a cast-iron pan and heat over medium-high heat. Using a slotted spoon, gently lower the leek into the hot oil. Fry for 1–2 minutes or until golden brown. Using the slotted spoon, remove and place them on the prepared baking sheet. Sprinkle with kosher salt. Remove and discard all but 2 tbsp oil from the pan. Turn off the heat but keep the pan on the stove; you'll use it for cooking the burgers shortly.

To make the burgers, place the ground chicken, mayo, breadcrumbs, garlic, green onions, chives, parsley, chili flakes, salt, and pepper in a medium mixing bowl and use your hands to combine. Do not overmix or your burgers will be tough: 10 seconds should do it. Divide the mixture into four equal portions and form them into patties.

Heat the oil left in the cast-iron pan over medium-high heat. Add two patties to the pan and cook undisturbed for about 6 minutes, then flip and continue to cook for 3 more minutes. Place a slice of Asiago on top of each patty, cover, lower the heat to medium-low, and continue to cook until the cheese has fully melted, about 2 minutes. The burgers are fully cooked when an instant-read thermometer registers 165°F. Remove from the pan and let rest for a few minutes. Repeat with the remaining two patties, adding a touch more oil if the pan seems too dry.

To assemble, divide the mayonnaise among the bottom halves of the toasted buns. Top with a slice or two of tomato, a cheesy burger, and a handful of crispy leeks. Finish with the top bun. Enjoy!

A Very Loud Burger, page 160

A Very Loud Burger

LAMB PATTY / BLUE CHEESE / RED ONION & BACON JAM / BRIOCHE

MAKES 4 BURGERS

RED ONION & BACON JAM

1 (12 oz/340 g) package bacon, chopped into small pieces (see note)

3 medium red onions, thinly sliced

2 cloves garlic, finely minced

1½ tsp dried oregano

½ cup dark brown sugar

½ cup apple cider vinegar

2 tbsp Dijon mustard

1 tbsp grainy mustard

½ tsp chili flakes

LAMB PATTIES

1½ lb (680 g) ground lamb

1 cup crumbled blue cheese (use your favorite—I like Gorgonzola)

2 tsp Worcestershire sauce

1 tsp kosher salt

1 tsp cracked black pepper

2 tbsp extra-virgin olive oil

ASSEMBLY

½ cup mayonnaise

4 brioche buns, sliced in half and toasted

4 pieces leaf lettuce

4 slices tomato

RECIPE PHOTO ON PAGE 158

NOTE

Don't let your bacon come to room temperature before you cut it. If you cut it directly from the fridge you'll have a much easier time slicing.

This burger has a lot to say, so listen up! It's sort of like it's screaming at you, but in an excellently gentle way. In this recipe, the seasoned lamb patty gets laced with blue cheese, which, as it cooks, melts into little pools of stinky cheese heaven. If this were as far as we took it, it would make me happy, but that's not how we do things here—we've added a red onion and bacon jam to top things off. The jam requires a bit of work, but it's worth it, and you'll have some left over to add to other sandwiches, eggs, or, heck, even a piece of grilled chicken or fish.

To make the jam, heat a large sauté pan over medium-high heat and add the chopped bacon. Cook, stirring every so often, until it crisps up, about 10–12 minutes. Remove the bacon to a bowl and transfer about half of the fat from the pan to a mug or bowl (see tips for using, opposite).

Reduce the heat to medium, add the onions to the pan, and sauté, occasionally stirring, until they have nicely softened, about 10 minutes. If you notice the bottom of the pan starting to burn slightly, add a splash of water and scrape down the pan with a wooden spoon. Add the garlic and oregano and continue to sauté for another few minutes. Add the brown sugar, vinegar, mustards, and chili flakes and bring the mixture to a boil. Reduce the heat to low, add the reserved bacon, and simmer for 35–40 minutes, stirring occasionally. At this point, the jam will have thickened nicely and can be set aside to cool. Once cool, this jam will keep in an airtight container in your fridge for up to 2 weeks.

Prep the burgers by placing the ground lamb, blue cheese, Worcestershire, salt, and pepper in a mixing bowl and use your hands to mix well. Be careful not to overmix, or your burgers will be tough—count to 10 as you mix and you'll be good to go. Divide into four equal portions and form into patties.

Heat half the oil in a cast-iron pan over medium-high heat. Cook the burgers, two at a time, for about 4–5 minutes on one side, then flip and cook for an additional 4–5 minutes on the other (for added confidence, check out the recommended temperature on page 144 and adjust cooking times accordingly). Add the remaining oil to the pan and repeat with the remaining patties.

To assemble, spread a generous amount of mayo on the four bottom halves of the buns and place a piece of lettuce and tomato on top. Top that with a burger patty, a tablespoon or two of the jam, and the top half of the bun. Enjoy!

WHAT TO DO WITH BACON FAT

The short answer is, don't throw it away! There are so many possible uses for bacon fat; here are just a few. Immediately strain the grease through a cheesecloth or coffee filter into a glass jar or container, let cool and then transfer to the fridge. Store in the fridge for up to 3 months and you can:

1 Use it to fry up some greens.

2 Substitute it for oil when popping popcorn.

3 Drizzle it over roasted veg.

4 Substitute it for butter when making a grilled cheese.

5 Use it to make a rich salad dressing.

6 Use it to fry your eggs.

7 Use it to make aioli; simply replace the oil in the aioli recipe with bacon grease.

8 Substitute it for butter in savory baking.

The Gaz

BEEF PATTY / MONTREAL SMOKED MEAT / CANDIED JALAPEÑO / SWEET & TANGY MAYO / RYE

MAKES 4 BURGERS

CANDIED JALAPEÑOS

1½ cups apple cider vinegar

1½ cups granulated sugar

1 tbsp brown mustard seeds

1½ tsp kosher salt

½ tsp garlic powder

½ tsp onion powder

¼ tsp ground turmeric

8–10 jalapeños, stems removed, sliced into rounds

Zest and juice of 1 lime

BEEF PATTIES

1½ lb (680 g) ground beef

2 cloves garlic, finely grated

2 tbsp finely chopped fresh flat-leaf parsley

1½ tsp Montreal steak spice or your favorite spice blend

2 tbsp extra-virgin olive oil

ASSEMBLY

1 recipe Sweet & Tangy Mayo (page 153)

8 slices rye, toasted

7 oz (200 g) Montreal smoked meat

NOTE

You'll need to make the jalapeños in advance because they need to cool to room temperature and then be refrigerated, preferably for a few days, to develop their flavor. However, if you can't wait, go ahead and make the burgers right away—you'll have extra for next time, I promise!

This is a messy burger; I'm not going to lie. Just look at it. But messy is good sometimes and can be especially rewarding for a burger. The candied jalapeños alone ooze with a sweet and spicy sauce that is hard not to love. If that wasn't enough, I've added a simple burger sauce to go along with it, because why not? Let's go all in with this one! The Montreal smoked meat adds a bit of smokiness and salt that round it all out.

Not all burgers need names, and not all names need burgers. But this burger required a name, a word I felt embodied what this burger stands for: saucy, spicy, sweet, and messy (in a good way, you know, like messy is good because it means you're spontaneous and care-free; also, fun fact, most geniuses are messy). No one could take up this moniker better than my dear friend Gaz (he's actually not a messy person, but he thoroughly enjoys a messy meal). So with that, I anoint this sandwich The Gaz, and I hope you think of him the next time you eat this burger and sauce is dripping down your chin.

We'll start by making the candied jalapeños. In a medium pot, combine the vinegar, sugar, mustard seeds, salt, garlic powder, onion powder, and turmeric. Set over medium-high heat and bring to a boil. Stir the mixture until all the sugar has dissolved, then add the jalapeños. Let the jalapeños cook in the boiling mixture for about 5 minutes. Use a slotted spoon to remove them and transfer to a clean jar.

Add the lime juice and let the liquid boil until it has reduced by half, about 15 minutes. Pour into the jar over the jalapeños and let cool to room temperature. Once cooled, stir in the lime zest, cover and refrigerate for up to 3 weeks.

To make the burgers, place the beef, garlic, parsley, and steak spice in a bowl and use your hands to mix; do not overmix or your burgers will be tough (count to 10 and you should be good!). Divide the mixture into four equal portions and shape them into patties.

Heat the oil in a cast-iron pan over medium-high heat. Cook two patties on one side for about 4–5 minutes, then flip and cook for another 4–5 minutes. Repeat with the remaining patties, adding a touch more oil if the pan seems dry. Check out the handy temperature guide on page 144, if you're curious about doneness temperatures. Remove the patties from the pan and you're ready to assemble.

To assemble, spread a generous amount of the mayo on four slices of toasted rye. Top with a patty, some candied jalapeños, and a handful of smoked meat. Finish with another slice of toasted rye and enjoy!

163

A Pickle Burger, for Lindsey

PORK PATTY / VINEGARY TOMATO / PICKLE MAYO / DILL PICKLES / PICKLE BUN

MAKES 4 BURGERS (WITH 4 LEFTOVER BUNS)

TOMATOES

2–3 firm tomatoes, sliced 1 inch thick

2 tbsp extra-virgin olive oil

2 tbsp apple cider vinegar

1 tsp dried dill weed

½ tsp kosher salt

½ tsp cracked black pepper

BUNS

2¼ tsp active dry yeast (one ¼ oz/8 g packet)

1 cup + 1 tbsp water warmed to approx. 105°F

2 tsp granulated sugar

⅓ cup unsalted butter, melted

1 large egg, beaten

3¼ cups all-purpose flour

1 tbsp dill weed

1 tsp kosher salt

1 egg yolk, beaten with 1 tsp whole milk

Dill weed, dill seeds, and sesame seeds (black or white or both)

PORK PATTIES

1½ lb (680 g) ground pork

1 tsp garlic powder

1 tsp dill weed

½ tsp kosher salt

½ tsp cracked black pepper

2 tbsp extra-virgin olive oil

4 slices extra-old white cheddar

PICKLE MAYO

½ cup mayonnaise

1 tsp pickle juice

1 dill pickle, finely minced

I created this burger for one of the hosts of *CTV Your Morning* and my friend, Lindsey Deluce. She was about to go on maternity leave with her third child, and the YM team wanted to send her off with some of her favorite foods. She told me that she had been craving pickles her entire pregnancy and was also obsessing over burgers. Easy—it had to be a pickle burger.

The other thing that Lindsey loves—pregnant or not—is tomatoes. So I decided to marinate some tomato slices and throw them in the mix. To top it all off we're finishing the burger with a simple pickle mayo. I've thrown in a recipe for some burger buns here too; they're loaded with dill and pair really well with this burger, but feel free to use store-bought. I'm telling you, if you love the flavor of anything pickled, this is the burger for you. And if you ever run into Lindsey, thank her for her love of pickles, burgers, and tomatoes— because this one is all her!

The tomatoes need a bit of time in the fridge, so let's get those out of the way first. Gently pile the slices into a medium-sized mixing bowl and make the vinaigrette. To a small mixing bowl add the olive oil, vinegar, dill weed, salt, and pepper and whisk until fully combined. Pour the vinaigrette over the tomato slices, cover with plastic wrap, and place in the fridge until the burgers are ready to assemble.

Time for the buns. To the bowl of a stand mixer fitted with the dough hook, add the yeast, sugar, and warm water. Let the mixture sit for 5 minutes, at which point the yeast will have started to wake up and bubble, and you know you're ready for the next step. Add the melted butter, egg, flour, dill weed, and salt and turn the mixer on to medium speed. Knead the dough for about 8 minutes; the dough will now be soft but slightly tacky. If you don't have a stand mixer, you can knead the dough by hand on a lightly floured work surface for about 10 minutes until the same consistency is achieved.

Place the dough in a large, lightly oiled mixing bowl, turning the dough a few times to coat, and cover with a tea towel. You'll want to find a slightly warm and cozy place for the dough to rise. It's ready for the next step when it has doubled in size, about an hour to an hour and a half.

Punch the dough down, remove it from the bowl, and divide it into eight equal pieces. Shape the pieces into balls and place them on a parchment-lined baking sheet. Cover them with a tea towel so they

CONTINUED

ASSEMBLY

A few handfuls of baby arugula

Dill pickles for serving

can rise a second time—a warm spot is preferable again—for about 30 minutes or until they double in size.

Preheat the oven to 375°F.

Brush the tops of the buns with the yolk mixture—make sure you get all the way down the sides—and sprinkle with dill weed, dill seeds, and sesame seeds.

Bake for 16–18 minutes or until golden brown. Set aside to cool.

For the burgers, in a bowl, use your hands to mix the ground pork, garlic powder, dill weed, salt, and pepper until combined, ensuring you do not overmix. Divide the meat mixture into four equal portions and form into patties. Ensure your grill is well oiled and preheat one side of it to high (375°F–400°F). Place the burgers on the side with direct heat and grill for about 2 minutes per side with the lid open. Flip the burgers onto the other side of the grill (with indirect heat) and continue to grill for another 3–4 minutes per side with the lid closed. Add the cheese, close the lid again, and continue to grill for an additional minute or until the cheese has fully melted. Remove from the grill and let rest for a few minutes before topping.

Before assembling, make the pickle mayo. In a small bowl, mix to combine the mayo, pickle juice, and minced pickle.

I prefer to toast my burger buns, but because these will have just come out of the oven and will be super fresh, use them as is. Toasting is best if you use them a day or two after baking.

To assemble, spread a generous amount of the pickle mayo onto the bottom halves of four buns. Top with a cheesy patty, some tomato slices, and a bit of arugula. Finish with the top bun, serve with dill pickles, and enjoy!

NOTE If grilling is not an option for you, follow the cooking instructions on the A Burger for Dad recipe opposite and fry your burgers instead.

A Burger for Dad

PORK PATTY / PEAR & RUM JAM / CREAM CHEESE / MASCARPONE / SMOKED HAM / BRIOCHE

MAKES 4 BURGERS

PEAR & RUM JAM

6 cups peeled, cored, and ½-inch-diced Bartlett pears

1 cup granulated sugar

1 cup packed dark brown sugar

Zest and juice of 1 lemon

2 tsp vanilla bean paste (if you don't have vanilla bean paste you can use vanilla extract)

⅓ cup dark rum (optional)

CHEESE

¼ cup cream cheese, softened

¼ cup mascarpone, softened

2 green onions, thinly sliced

½ tsp kosher salt

PORK PATTIES

1½ lb (680 g) ground pork

2 cloves garlic, finely grated

¼ cup finely chopped fresh flat-leaf parsley

2 tbsp finely chopped fresh sage

1 tsp Worcestershire sauce

½ tsp kosher salt

1 tsp cracked black pepper

2 tbsp extra-virgin olive oil

ASSEMBLY

4 brioche buns, toasted

12–16 pieces thinly sliced smoked ham

RECIPE PHOTO ON PAGE 168

NOTE

If you're not in the mood to make jam, buy some! Apricot jam is a good substitute if you can't find pear jam.

This burger is pretty special to me, as it includes a recipe that is close to my family's hearts. As I've written about on page 105, my dad spent a lot of time in the kitchen, especially later in his life. He loved to cook, but specialized in soups and jams, of all things.

I've paired his pear and rum jam with this burger, along with some smoky ham and a delightful combination of mascarpone and cream cheese. When I say this burger will bring all the boys to the yard, I'm not kidding. Add a milkshake and you'll guarantee a yard full of boys. If you don't get the reference, ask your kids. Milkshakes and yards and boys aside, I think my dad would have really loved this burger.

To make the jam, combine the pears, both sugars, and the lemon zest and juice in a large pot or Dutch oven and mix well. Set over medium-high heat, let the sugars melt, and bring to a boil. Let the mixture boil, stirring often to prevent sticking or burning, for 10 minutes.

Reduce the heat to low and let simmer for 25 minutes, stirring occasionally. As the mixture thickens, add the vanilla and the dark rum (if using). Stir well to incorporate. If you like your jam fairly chunky, leave it as is. If you prefer something less chunky, use a potato masher to mash it to your heart's desire. Set aside to let cool. The jam can be kept in the fridge for up to 2 weeks or in the freezer for up to a year.

And now for the easiest part of this recipe, the cheese. Place all the ingredients in a bowl and mix to combine. Cover and refrigerate until needed.

To make the patties, place the pork, garlic, parsley, sage, Worcestershire, salt, and pepper in a bowl and use your hands to mix well (do not overmix, as it will make for tough burgers; the mixture should still have a slightly loose texture. If you press it too much, the burgers can become dense when cooked.). Divide the mixture into four equal portions and shape them into patties.

Heat the oil in a pan over medium-high heat. Cook the burgers for about 4–5 minutes on one side, flip, and cook for another 4–5 minutes or until nicely browned on both sides and an instant-read thermometer registers 160°F when inserted into the center of the burger. Remove from the pan and let rest for a few minutes before assembling.

To assemble the burgers, spread some of the cheese mixture on the bottom of each bun. Top with a patty, spread a few tablespoons of jam on top, and add some slices of ham. Finish with the top bun and enjoy!

167

A Better Turkey Burger

TURKEY PATTY / CRANBERRY, APPLE & ORANGE CHUTNEY / BRIOCHE

MAKES 4 BURGERS

CRANBERRY, APPLE & ORANGE CHUTNEY

1 cup granulated sugar

¼ cup apple cider vinegar

2 tbsp water

2 cups cranberries, fresh or frozen

1 apple, peeled, cored, and cut into ¼-inch cubes

Zest and juice of 1 orange

¼ tsp chili flakes

½ tsp kosher salt

TURKEY PATTIES

1½ lb (680 g) ground turkey

¼ cup dried breadcrumbs

¼ cup mayonnaise

½ cup shredded mozzarella

1 tbsp chopped fresh sage

1 large egg, whisked

1 tbsp Worcestershire sauce

1 tsp smoked paprika

½ tsp ground ginger

1 tsp kosher salt

1 tsp cracked black pepper

2 tbsp extra-virgin olive oil

ASSEMBLY

4 brioche buns, sliced in half and toasted

⅓ cup mayonnaise

Green leaf lettuce

Turkey burgers typically get a pretty bad rap. And deservedly so, because they can be relatively dry, tough, and crumbly. Sounds great, doesn't it? What ground turkey lacks is fat. Fat is what beef and pork have that turkey has so little of. Turkey is naturally lean, so all you need to do is help it out a bit. Adding mayonnaise and grated mozzarella to the mix will help the burger stay moist and juicy when grilled.

I added a cranberry, apple, and orange chutney to the burger because, let's be honest, cranberry and turkey are a match made in heaven; like peanut butter and jam, macaroni and cheese, bacon and eggs, or RuPaul and drag, they're just better together. So go ahead and make this for a casual Thanksgiving or in the middle of the damn summer; I think you'll love it any time of year.

Let's make the chutney first. In a large saucepan over medium-high heat, combine the sugar, cider vinegar, and water and stir until the sugar has dissolved. Add the cranberries, apple, orange zest and juice, chili flakes, and salt. Bring the mixture to a boil, then reduce the heat to medium-low and let simmer for 25 minutes, stirring occasionally. Remove the chutney from the heat and let it cool slightly. If you allow the mixture to cool completely, warm it and loosen with a bit of water before serving.

For the turkey patties, place everything except the oil in a large bowl and mix well. Form into four equal-sized patties and place them on a small baking sheet or plate lined with parchment paper. Chill in the fridge for 30–45 minutes to firm up.

Once the patties have firmed up, you're ready to go. Heat about 1 tbsp oil in a cast-iron pan over medium heat. Add two patties at a time and let cook undisturbed for 5–6 minutes. Flip and continue to cook for an additional 5–6 minutes. Turkey burgers are done when the internal temperature reaches 165°F. Add the remaining oil to the pan and repeat with the remaining patties.

To assemble, slather the bottom halves of the buns with some mayo and top each with leaf lettuce, a juicy patty, and some chutney. Finish with the top half of the bun and enjoy!

The Fish Burger

MAPLE MUSTARD HALIBUT / FENNEL SLAW / LEMON TARTAR SAUCE / CIABATTA

MAKES 4 BURGERS

FENNEL SLAW

1 bulb fennel, trimmed and very thinly sliced (a mandoline is helpful here)

¼ small head purple cabbage, shredded

1 small red onion, thinly sliced

2 tbsp roughly chopped fresh flat-leaf parsley

2 tbsp roughly chopped fresh cilantro

2 tbsp roughly chopped fresh chives

½ jalapeño, finely minced (seeds removed for less heat)

Juice of 2 limes (about ¼ cup)

1 tbsp runny honey

2 tbsp extra-virgin olive oil

½ tsp kosher salt

½ tsp cracked black pepper

LEMON TARTAR SAUCE

¼ cup mayonnaise

¼ cup Greek yogurt

1 shallot, finely minced

1 clove garlic, finely grated

1 dill pickle, finely minced

1 tbsp capers, chopped

1 tbsp chopped fresh dill

1 tsp grainy mustard

Zest of ½ lemon

½ tsp cracked black pepper

MAPLE MUSTARD HALIBUT

2 tbsp grainy mustard

1 tbsp maple syrup

4 (6 oz/170 g) skinless, fresh halibut fillets

1 tbsp extra-virgin olive oil

ASSEMBLY

4 ciabatta buns, sliced in half and toasted

Is this really a burger? Hell, yeah! A hamburger is defined as a patty of ground beef, and a burger is described as a sandwich similar to a hamburger. So there you have it: anything can be a burger! I wanted a fish burger in this chapter, and I chose to use halibut because of its mild and sweet characteristics. Then I jazzed up the halibut with some mustard and a touch of maple syrup. They work nicely together and will caramelize in the pan just before the fish is done. Halibut is, however, a fish that tends to overcook quite quickly, so be sure to keep an eye on it while cooking.

Along with a few other ingredients (I'm looking at you, mortadella and eggplant), fennel appears a few times throughout this book, and I'm so happy about that. Fennel is one of those vegetables that's delicious when raw, like in this slaw, but also really wonderful when pickled (see A Cuban Sandwich, page 181) and entirely different when roasted (see It's Another Grilled Cheese, page 130).

Start by making the slaw. In a large mixing bowl, combine the fennel, cabbage, onion, parsley, cilantro, chives, jalapeño, lime juice, honey, olive oil, salt, and pepper. Toss to coat. Cover and refrigerate until needed.

Like most of the sauces in this book, this tartar sauce is super simple. In a bowl, whisk together all the ingredients, then cover and refrigerate until needed. This sauce will keep covered in the fridge for up to a week.

To make the fish burgers, place the mustard and maple syrup in a small bowl and whisk to combine. Spread onto one side of each of the four pieces of fish. Heat the oil in a large cast-iron pan over medium-high heat. Add the fish, coated side up, two pieces at a time, and cook for about 3–4 minutes. Flip and continue to cook for an additional 3–4 minutes. The fillets are done when opaque and flake easily with a fork.

To assemble, spread a generous amount of the tartar sauce onto the bottom halves of the toasted buns. Place a piece of halibut on top and a good handful of slaw on top of that. Close with the top bun. Enjoy!

HOT HOT MESS

The sandwiches in this chapter are my idea of comfort food. I mean, I think all sandwiches are comforting food, but these feel extra comforting to me. Wikipedia describes comfort food as "food that provides a nostalgic or sentimental value to someone, and may be characterized by its high caloric nature, high carbohydrate level or simple preparation." Sounds like a sandwich to me! In this chapter, you'll go on a journey all over the world—from France to the American South, from New York City to Cuba, and all the way to Pakistan—with my spin on sandwiches that you may or may not have heard of . . . yet.

A SAUSAGE SANDWICH

ANDOUILLE / SWEET POTATO / SPINACH / FRESH HERB & LEMON MAYO / BAGUETTE

MAKES 4 SANDWICHES

SWEET POTATOES

2 sweet potatoes, sliced into
¼-inch planks

1 tsp sweet paprika

1 tsp ground cumin

½ tsp garlic powder

1 tsp kosher salt

1 tsp cracked black pepper

¼ cup extra-virgin olive oil

FRESH HERB & LEMON MAYO

½ cup mayonnaise

2 tbsp finely chopped fresh flat-
leaf parsley

2 tbsp finely chopped fresh basil

2 green onions, finely chopped

Zest of 1 lemon

½ tsp kosher salt

½ tsp cracked black pepper

ASSEMBLY

1 baguette (I use a rye baguette),
sliced into four 5–6-inch pieces
and split down the middle

2 andouille sausages, grilled (see
page 37) and sliced

Fresh spinach

There are many variations of the andouille sausage, particularly in France, where it is thought to have originated (although some folks believe it was invented in Germany). French andouille is made of pork, makes good use of the intestine, and is heavily spiced and smoked. When the Acadians made their way to Louisiana in the mid to late 1700s, they brought their version of andouille sausage, a bit spicier than some of the others found in France. It has evolved since then and doesn't resemble its French cousin much anymore. The Cajun andouille generally uses pork shoulder and is powerfully spicy, rich, and fatty, but without the use of offal. Most North American grocery stores and butchers carry the Cajun version of andouille sausage, but you can find the French version at specialized shops and butchers, and I encourage you to try it if you can find it. If you're having a hard time finding any type of andouille sausage, feel free to substitute here with chorizo or even spicy Italian sausage. Although nothing is a perfect substitute, those will still give this sandwich the spice and richness it needs.

Preheat the oven to 400°F and line two baking sheets with parchment paper.

For the sweet potatoes, in a large mixing bowl, carefully toss the sweet potatoes with the paprika, cumin, garlic powder, salt, pepper, and olive oil. Place on the prepared baking sheets and roast for 20 minutes, flipping halfway through, or until tender and slightly charred.

To make the fresh herb and lemon mayo, place all the ingredients in a bowl, mix well, and set aside.

To assemble, spread a generous amount of mayo onto the bottom of each baguette piece, then top with sweet potato, sausage slices, and some fresh spinach. Close the sandwiches with the top slices of baguette and enjoy!

A CUBAN SANDWICH

PORK / PICKLED FENNEL / HOMEMADE GRAINY MUSTARD / GRUYÈRE / HAM / BRIOCHE

MAKES 4 SANDWICHES

GRAINY MUSTARD

⅓ cup yellow mustard seeds

⅓ cup brown mustard seeds

½ cup apple cider vinegar

½ cup water

2 tbsp brown sugar

1 tsp kosher salt

PICKLED FENNEL

1 cup water

1 cup apple cider vinegar

1 tbsp granulated sugar

1 tbsp kosher salt

½ tsp chili flakes

1 bulb fennel, trimmed, cored, and thinly sliced

PORK TENDERLOIN

3 tbsp extra-virgin olive oil

3 cloves garlic, finely minced

2 tbsp brown sugar

1 tsp dry mustard

1 tsp fennel seeds

1 tsp smoked paprika

1 tsp cracked black pepper

½ tsp kosher salt

1 pork tenderloin, trimmed and silver skin removed

ASSEMBLY

4 tbsp mayonnaise

½ cup grainy mustard

4 brioche buns, sliced in half

12 slices Black Forest ham

8 slices Gruyère

1 tbsp extra-virgin olive oil

Many years ago, I went on a cruise with some friends through the Caribbean. I had never really dreamed of going on a cruise or even pictured myself on one. But sometimes you must roll with things and tell yourself that you will have fun. It turns out that I did have fun—some nights were a bit too much fun. Let's say the tequila and rum were flowing, and if you've been on a cruise, you know what I mean. That's where the Cuban sandwich comes into play. You see, there was this little café high up on one of the decks that few knew stayed open late. I stumbled upon it on the first night after too many tequila shots and quite a bit of dancing. The guy behind the counter insisted he make me a Cuban sandwich—he could tell I needed it! And so began a tradition. Every night, he would make me a Cuban and I would sit and savor this joyously salty pork sandwich with melty cheese and briny pickles. I looked forward to it every day; it was probably my favorite part of the cruise.

I've never been on a cruise again, but I've made this sandwich a lot, and I swear I never get sick of it. It appeared at the inaugural sandwich party I had in the UK, and so did a few stories of my time on that cruise. Let's say that if you ever run into me, I may be coaxed into telling you a few, but until then, all you get is this very delicious recipe.

You'll need to start the mustard and the pickled fennel the day before—but don't fret, they're both minimal work (and if time doesn't allow, feel free to use store-bought grainy mustard and pickles instead, I won't tell).

For the mustard, place all the ingredients in a jar, seal, and shake well. Place the jar on the counter overnight to allow the mustard seeds to soak.

Once soaked, pour the contents of the jar into a blender and blend for a few minutes. And you're done! See, fancy grainy mustard made by you in no time! The mustard can be stored in an airtight container in the fridge for up to 2 months.

To make the pickled fennel, start by making the brine. In a medium saucepan over high heat, combine the water, vinegar, sugar, salt, and chili flakes and bring to a boil. Stir until the sugar and salt are dissolved. Place the sliced fennel in a large mason jar and pour the hot brine overtop. Set it on the counter to come to room temperature, and then pop it in the fridge to chill and pickle overnight. Any extra

CONTINUED

pickled fennel can be stored in the fridge for up to 1 month, and it's not only great on sandwiches but also in salads or just to snack on.

For the pork, preheat the oven to 400°F.

In a small mixing bowl, whisk to combine 2 tbsp of the olive oil and the garlic, brown sugar, dry mustard, fennel seeds, smoked paprika and set aside. Pat the tenderloin dry with a paper towel and season with salt and pepper.

Heat the remaining 1 tbsp olive oil in a cast-iron pan over medium-high heat until the oil shimmers. Sear the tenderloin until nicely browned on all sides, about 5–6 minutes. Remove from the heat and brush with the olive oil mixture, coating the whole tenderloin evenly. Place the cast-iron pan in the oven and roast for 15–20 minutes or until an instant-read thermometer inserted into the thickest part of the pork reads 145°F. Remove from the oven and tent with foil. When ready to assemble, remove the foil and slice the pork thinly.

Sandwich-making time! Preheat the oven to 450°F, line a baking sheet with foil, and brush with oil. Spread the mayo and grainy mustard on the bottom of each bun and top with pork slices, three pieces of ham, a generous amount of pickled fennel, and two slices of Gruyère. Spread a bit more mustard on the cut side of the top bun as well, and place on top of the sandwich.

Place the sandwiches on the prepared baking sheet and brush the tops with olive oil. Cover with a second baking sheet and place a brick or cast-iron pan on top to weigh it down. Place in the oven for 6 minutes or until the cheese is completely melted.

Remove from the oven and enjoy!

A GARLIC CHICKEN SANDWICH

CHICKEN / PICKLED ONIONS / PROSCIUTTO / ROASTED GARLIC SAUCE / TOMATO / BAGUETTE

MAKES 6 SANDWICHES

PICKLED RED ONIONS

1 cup apple cider vinegar

1 cup water

1 tbsp kosher salt

1 tsp granulated sugar

1 tsp chili flakes (optional)

1 red onion, thinly sliced

ROASTED GARLIC SAUCE

2 heads garlic

1 tbsp extra-virgin olive oil

1 tsp kosher salt

1 tsp cracked black pepper

2 tbsp unsalted butter

2 tbsp all-purpose flour

1 cup whole milk

½ cup finely grated Asiago

CHICKEN

6 large skinless, boneless chicken thighs

1 tsp smoked paprika

1 tsp kosher salt

1 tsp cracked black pepper

3 tbsp extra-virgin olive oil

ASSEMBLY

12 slices prosciutto

1 baguette, sliced into 6 pieces, split down the middle, and toasted

3 tomatoes, sliced

Frisée

This recipe came about when I was asked to do an anti–Valentine's Day segment on the TV show *CTV Your Morning*. My producer Shannon and I thought it would be fun to lean into the idea of things that would not necessarily be on the menu for a typical Valentine's Day dinner. Garlic and sandwiches were tops on that list (stinky and messy!), and this sandwich was born. Roasting the garlic takes away its natural bite and instead serves up a bit of sweetness that lends well to the sauce's richness. This sandwich almost feels like a huge hug, enveloping you with each bite. I tend to make it during the colder months when I feel like something comforting and rich, but like any sandwich, it's delicious any time of year.

First up, let's pickle those onions. Add the vinegar and water to a medium pot over medium-high heat and bring to a gentle simmer. Add the salt and sugar and mix until dissolved. Place the onion and chili flakes (if using) in a bowl and pour the brine overtop. Leave the bowl on the counter to cool to room temperature. The onions you don't use can be stored in a jar or airtight container in the fridge for up to 1 month.

While the onions are cooling, let's roast the garlic for the sauce. Preheat the oven to 350°F. Cut the tops off the garlic bulbs exposing the tips of the cloves. Discard the tops and place the bulbs on a piece of foil. Coat the garlic with olive oil and season each with ½ tsp salt and ½ tsp pepper. Wrap them both tightly into a package and place on a baking sheet. Roast in the oven for 40 minutes. Carefully unwrap the garlic and set aside to cool.

Next up is the chicken. Pat the thighs dry with a paper towel and season with paprika, salt, and pepper. Heat the oil in a medium skillet over medium-high heat. Place the chicken in the preheated skillet and cook undisturbed for 6 minutes. Flip and cook for 6 minutes more or until they are no longer pink in the middle; an instant-read thermometer will read 165°F when the thighs are done. Once cooled enough to work with, cut the thighs in half lengthwise and set aside.

Continue with the garlic sauce. Squeeze out the roasted garlic cloves into a small bowl. Mash until smooth, taking in the sweet and slightly caramel scent that's sure to be filling your kitchen.

CONTINUED

Melt the butter in a medium pot over medium heat. Once melted, add the flour and whisk to combine. Slowly pour in the milk and whisk until the sauce has thickened, about 5–6 minutes. Add the roasted garlic, Asiago, and the remaining ½ tsp salt and ½ tsp pepper, and continue to whisk until smooth. Remove from heat.

Time to crisp up the prosciutto. Add four slices of the prosciutto to a nonstick pan over high heat and dry-fry until crisp. Flip and dry-fry the other side until crisp. Transfer the fried prosciutto to a plate and set aside. Repeat with the remaining prosciutto.

To assemble, slather a good amount of the sauce onto the top and bottom slices of the baguette. Top with tomato slices, some frisée, and two pieces of chicken. Finish with some fried prosciutto and the top piece of baguette.

IT'S A HAWAIIAN PIZZA SANDWICH!

MORTADELLA / GRILLED PINEAPPLE / TOMATO SAUCE / MOZZARELLA / PROVOLONE / BRIOCHE

MAKES 4 SANDWICHES

TOMATO SAUCE

1 tbsp extra-virgin olive oil

½ small yellow onion, minced

2 cloves garlic, finely minced

½ tsp kosher salt

½ tsp smoked paprika

½ tsp dried oregano

Pinch of chili flakes

1 cup passata

1 tbsp brown sugar

1 tbsp apple cider vinegar

PINEAPPLE

4 pineapple rings about ½ to 1 inch thick

2 tbsp extra-virgin olive oil

Flaky salt

ASSEMBLY

4 brioche buns, cut in half

4 slices mozzarella

4 slices provolone

24 thin slices mortadella

It's no secret that I love mortadella—it makes its way into more recipes in this book than most people think it deserves. But that's okay; I'm not ashamed of my love for this porky pleasure. Many people compare it to American bologna, but nothing could be further from the truth. Whereas American bologna is made of emulsified pork and fat, mortadella is made by combining pork and chunks of fat. The chunks of fat are what give mortadella its iconic spotted look. Add specks of black pepper and sometimes pieces of pistachio or even olives, and it's clear that this is no ordinary lunch meat. Sliced thin, the almost buttery texture lends itself well to a sandwich—but don't forget to include it on your next charcuterie board as well; it's sure to be a hit.

I came up with this sandwich as a sort of ode to a very Canadian invention: the Hawaiian pizza. I love the salty-sweet combination of ham and pineapple that a slice of Hawaiian pizza has. But I wanted to replace the ham with something else, and there was no other option. The salty, smooth mortadella combined with the sweet grilled pineapple is a win-win. Add to that some spicy tomato sauce, melted mozzarella and provolone, and a pillowy brioche bun, and you've got a pretty great sandwich. I hope you agree.

Begin by making the tomato sauce. Heat the olive oil in a medium saucepan over medium-high heat. Add the onion and cook until softened. Add the garlic, salt, smoked paprika, oregano, and chili flakes and continue to cook for another minute or so. Add the passata, brown sugar, and apple cider vinegar. Bring to a boil and then reduce the heat and simmer for 10 minutes, stirring frequently. Remove from the heat and set aside.

Turning to the pineapple, heat a cast-iron pan over high heat and brush each pineapple ring with oil. Sear the rings for 3 minutes per side. Remove from the pan and sprinkle with flaky salt.

Preheat the oven to broil and line two baking sheets with foil.

To assemble, spread both halves of the brioche buns with a few tablespoons of tomato sauce and place on the prepared baking sheet. Top the bottom bun with mozzarella and the top bun with provolone. Broil the buns until the cheese is melted and bubbling. Remove from the oven, place a pineapple ring on the bottom bun, and top with a pile of mortadella. Close the sandwich and enjoy!

(OR "THE I KNOW HALF OF YOU WILL TURN YOUR NOSES UP AT THIS SANDWICH, BUT I DON'T CARE" SANDWICH)

MARBELLA

CHICKEN / DATE / FIG / OLIVE / MAPLE SYRUP / CIABATTA

MAKES 6 SANDWICHES

CHICKEN

2 tbsp extra-virgin olive oil

6 skin-on, bone-in chicken thighs

1 tsp kosher salt

1 tsp cracked black pepper

FILLING

2 tbsp extra-virgin olive oil

½ red onion, thinly sliced

4 cloves garlic, minced

¼ cup capers

6 Medjool dates, pitted and halved

5 fresh figs, quartered

½ cup pitted black olives

½ cup pitted green olives

2 tbsp red wine vinegar

1 tsp dried oregano

½ tsp cracked black pepper

½ cup roughly chopped fresh flat-leaf parsley

ASSEMBLY

6 ciabatta buns, sliced in half, toasted

This sandwich was inspired by the iconic Chicken Marbella, that famous dish created in New York City in the late 1970s. Sheila Lukins and Julee Rosso started the hugely successful Silver Palate, a take-away food shop that spun into a mini empire with three massively successful cookbooks that took America by storm. Their recipe for Chicken Marbella appeared in one of the books and quickly became a staple of the American dinner party. Flash forward to today: it is still quite popular and (unlike its culinary cousins of the '80s) has managed to age pretty well. I love the sweetness and texture that the dates and figs bring to this recipe, and the brininess of the olives and capers balances things out perfectly.

Preheat the oven to 425°F.

We'll start with the chicken. Heat the oil in a cast-iron pan over medium-high heat. Pat down the chicken thighs with a paper towel and season with salt and pepper. Sear the thighs, skin side down, for about 6–7 minutes. Flip the chicken—the skin should easily release from the pan, but if it's sticking, continue to sear for a few more minutes. Pop the pan into the oven to cook for another 15–17 minutes, or until an instant-read thermometer inserted into the thickest part of the thigh reads 165°F. Remove from the oven and set aside to cool slightly.

While the chicken is in the oven, start the filling. Heat the oil in a large sauté pan over medium-high heat. Add the onion and sauté for 5 minutes then add the garlic and continue to sauté for 2 more minutes. Add the capers, dates, figs, and olives and continue to sauté for a few more minutes. Next, add the vinegar and oregano and season with pepper. Turn the heat to low and simmer until you're ready to add the chicken and parsley.

Once the chicken is cool enough to handle, remove the meat and crispy skin from the bones, roughly chop the skin, and add it to the filling along with the parsley. Mix thoroughly, and you're ready for assembly!

To assemble, spoon a generous amount of chicken and filling onto the bottom half of each ciabatta bun and sandwich it closed. Be warned, this one could get messy.

RAGÙ FOR YOU

BEEF & PORK RAGÙ / CHARRED BROCCOLINI / MOZZARELLA / ITALIAN LOAF

MAKES 6–8 SANDWICHES

RAGÙ

1 tbsp unsalted butter

6 oz (170 g) cubed pancetta

1 yellow onion, finely chopped

2 carrots, finely chopped

2 stalks celery, finely chopped

1 tsp cracked black pepper

1 lb (454 g) ground beef

1 lb (454 g) ground pork

1 cup white wine

2 cups beef stock

⅓ cup tomato paste

Pinch of ground nutmeg

1 cup whole milk

CHARRED BROCCOLINI

1 bunch broccolini, trimmed and halved

1 tbsp extra-virgin olive oil

1 tsp chili flakes

1 tsp kosher salt

ASSEMBLY

12–16 slices Italian loaf, toasted

Extra-virgin olive oil

1½ cups shredded mozzarella

The Italian ragù—the luscious, flavorsome and always rewarding sauce—is one of the more famous dishes within the Italian culinary world. We could write a whole chapter on its origin story, but we don't have time for that (we have sandwiches to make!) so here's a little primer. Whether we're speaking of the version from the northern city of Bologna (*ragù alla Bolognese*), or the one from the southern city of Naples (*ragù alla Napoletana*), while slightly different onto themselves, they both derive from the French dish *ragoût*. While no one can say exactly when ragoût found its way onto the Italian culinary scene and morphed into ragù, it is believed to have been around since at least the Renaissance period, when the ruling class would enjoy it as a regular part of their meals. The version you are about to make is based on ragù alla Bolognese and I hope you enjoy it as much as I do. Give yourself some time to make this; like the best ragùs, this is not a quick weeknight event!

Start by making the ragù. Melt the butter in a heavy-bottomed pot over medium-high heat. Add the pancetta and cook, stirring occasionally, until nicely browned and the fat has rendered, about 6–8 minutes.

Add the onion, carrots, and celery, season with the pepper, and continue to cook until the vegetables have softened nicely, another 6–8 minutes.

Add the ground meat, break it up with a wooden spoon, and continue cooking for 7–8 minutes, occasionally stirring and scraping the bottom of the pot. Once the meat has browned, add the wine and stir. Let it come to a boil and cook for about 5 minutes, then add the beef stock, tomato paste, and nutmeg. Reduce the heat to low and let simmer, uncovered, for 1½ hours, stirring occasionally.

Add the milk to a small saucepan and bring to a simmer. Slowly pour the hot milk into the ragù and stir until incorporated. Cover the sauce and let simmer for 45 minutes more, stirring every 15 minutes.

While the ragù is simmering, prepare the broccolini. Preheat the oven to 475°F and line a baking sheet with parchment paper. Place the broccolini on the prepared baking sheet, drizzle with the olive oil, and sprinkle with chili flakes and kosher salt. Roast for 20 minutes or until nicely charred. Set aside.

Time to assemble: Turn the oven to broil, arrange half of the toasted bread on the prepared baking sheet, and drizzle with a bit of olive oil. Scoop a generous amount of ragù onto the slices, top with a few pieces of charred broccolini, and sprinkle with the mozzarella. Broil until the mozzarella has melted, about 1 minute. Remove from the oven, top with the remaining toasted bread, and enjoy!

THE BIG DIPPER

CRISPY FRIED MUSHROOM / MUSHROOM JUS / SHALLOT CHILI BUTTER / CRUSTY ROLL

MAKES 6 SANDWICHES

MUSHROOM JUS

1 tbsp extra-virgin olive oil

2 carrots, chopped

1 medium onion, chopped

Kosher salt and cracked black pepper

2 cloves garlic, sliced

2 tbsp tomato paste

7 oz (200 g) cremini mushrooms, sliced

1 oz (15 g) dried shiitake mushrooms

1 sprig fresh sage

5 cups of water

SHALLOT CHILI BUTTER

½ cup unsalted butter, softened

1 shallot, finely minced

1 tsp kosher salt

1 tsp cracked black pepper

½–1 tsp chili flakes (depending on your spice preference)

2 tbsp finely chopped fresh flat-leaf parsley

CRISPY FRIED MUSHROOMS

2½ cups all-purpose flour

1½ cups buttermilk

2 tbsp cornstarch

1 tsp dried oregano

1 tsp kosher salt

½ tsp garlic powder

½ tsp onion powder

½ tsp sweet paprika

½ tsp cracked black pepper

8 cups neutral oil for frying, such as grapeseed or sunflower

10½ oz (300 g) oyster mushrooms

Flaky salt

The idea for this sandwich came to me while I was researching classic sandwiches. The French dip has been around since the early 1900s, invented by one of two Los Angeles restaurants, depending on whom you believe. It's a hot sandwich usually composed of thinly sliced beef nestled into a French roll or baguette. And that's where the "French" in French dip comes from—the bread, not because of any relation to France.

I wanted to take this concept and put a different spin on it. I love the meatiness of mushrooms and thought I could create a vegetarian sandwich in a style that hasn't been overdone. I think this one delivers. The crispy fried mushrooms sit on a bed of savory and slightly spicy butter that melts somewhat when the mushrooms get nestled on top. And the crusty rolls work perfectly with the crispy mushrooms when dipped into the mushroom jus. It's a sandwich that checks a lot of boxes.

We're going to start by making the mushroom jus. Heat the oil in a large pot over medium-high heat. Add the carrots and onion, season with salt and pepper, and sauté for 5 minutes. Add the garlic and tomato paste and continue to sauté for 1 minute. Add the fresh and dried mushrooms, sage, and water and bring the mixture to a boil, then reduce the heat to low and simmer for 45 minutes. Remove from the heat and strain the liquid, discarding the vegetables and herbs. Return the liquid to the pot, adjust the seasoning if needed, and turn the heat to low to keep warm while you make the mushrooms and butter. The simmering jus will envelop your kitchen with the warmest of hugs—enjoy it.

Next is the shallot chili butter. Mix all the ingredients in a small bowl until well combined. Set aside but do not refrigerate. Any leftover butter can be stored in an airtight container in the fridge for a few weeks.

Next up, the crispy fried mushrooms. Line a baking sheet with paper towels and place a wire rack on top.

Place 1 cup flour in a bowl, pour in the buttermilk, and whisk to combine until no lumps remain. In a second bowl, combine the remaining flour, cornstarch, oregano, salt, garlic powder, onion powder, paprika, and pepper and whisk to combine.

Heat the oil to 350°F in a heavy-bottomed pot over medium-high heat. Coat the mushrooms in the dry flour mixture and then dip them in the buttermilk mixture, ensuring the whole mushroom is covered.

ASSEMBLY

6 crusty rolls, cut in half and toasted

Chopped fresh thyme

Carefully place them back in the dry flour mixture and press it onto them to coat.

Fry the mushrooms in the hot oil for 2 minutes, then flip and fry for 2 more minutes. Remove to the prepared baking sheet and sprinkle with flaky salt.

To assemble, generously butter the toasted buns with the shallot chili butter and nestle in two to three fried mushrooms. Sprinkle with chopped thyme and serve with a warm bowl of mushroom jus for dipping. Enjoy!

THE NIK T & AMBER J

COCONUT FRIED SMELT / CITRUS GINGER MAYO / KALE / CRUSTY ROLL

MAKES 4 SANDWICHES

CITRUS GINGER MAYO

½ cup mayonnaise

Zest of 1 lemon

Zest of 1 lime

Zest of ½ grapefruit

½-inch knob fresh ginger, finely grated

SMELTS

1 cup all-purpose flour

½ cup cornstarch

1½ tsp kosher salt

1 tsp cracked black pepper

Zest and juice of 1 lemon

2 large eggs

1½ cups unsweetened shredded coconut

½ cup panko

Neutral oil for frying, such as grapeseed or sunflower

1 lb (454 g) fresh smelts cleaned

Flaky salt

KALE

2 cups roughly chopped kale leaves (stems removed)

1 tsp extra-virgin olive oil

½ tsp kosher salt

ASSEMBLY

4 crusty rolls, cut in half

NOTE

Before you zest any citrus, give it a rinse.

Fried smelts might not be the first thing you think of when thinking about sandwiches, and I don't blame you. But hear me out: when fried, these little guys turn into sandwich gold! My friends Nik and Amber, for whom this sandwich is named, turned me on to the joys of smelts. They're more widely available than you might think; they are found in the North Atlantic and North Pacific oceans, as well as lakes, streams, and rivers all over Europe, North America, and Northeast Asia. You're likely to find them in the frozen seafood section of the grocery store, or if you're lucky, you might catch them at the fresh seafood counter of your favorite fishmonger.

This is a play on coconut shrimp, a favorite of mine growing up. I think swapping out the shrimp for smelts is a fun way not only to try new seafood but to eat something that is very sustainable and affordable. Kale, everyone's favorite superfood, adds a kick of freshness to the sandwich, and the citrus ginger mayo does a great job of finishing things off.

Let's go ahead and make the mayo straightaway and get that over with. Place all the ingredients in a bowl and mix well until thoroughly combined and smooth. Cover and refrigerate until needed.

For the smelts, begin by preparing the dredging station. In one bowl, mix to combine the flour, cornstarch, salt, pepper, and lemon zest. In another bowl, whisk the eggs. In a final bowl, mix together the coconut and panko.

Heat 3 inches of oil in a heavy-bottomed pot over medium heat to 350°F. Line a baking sheet with paper towels and place a wire rack on top.

Dredge the fish first in the flour mixture, then in the egg, and finally in the coconut mixture. Shake off any excess. Fry in batches for about 4 minutes per batch, turning every 30 seconds. Remove to the wire rack, sprinkle with flaky salt, and drizzle with a bit of lemon juice. Repeat until all the fish are fried.

Before assembling the sandwich, toss the kale leaves with the oil and salt and massage for 2 to 3 minutes to soften slightly.

To assemble, spread a generous amount of the mayo on the insides of the rolls. Top the bottom halves with a generous amount of fried smelts and some kale, and finish with the top buns. Enjoy!

ANOTHER CHICKEN SANDWICH

CURRY ROASTED CHICKEN / TOMATO CUMIN SALAD /
WHIPPED CINNAMON MAPLE BUTTER / BAGUETTE

MAKES 4 BIGGER OR 6 SMALLER SANDWICHES

WHIPPED CINNAMON MAPLE BUTTER

½ cup unsalted butter, softened

2 tbsp dark maple syrup

1 tsp ground cinnamon

½ tsp kosher salt

TOMATO CUMIN SALAD

4 small tomatoes, cut into small wedges

1 shallot, thinly sliced

1 clove garlic, minced

½ tsp ground cumin

½ tsp kosher salt

½ tsp cracked black pepper

1 tbsp extra-virgin olive oil

Juice of ½ lemon

CURRY ROASTED CHICKEN

4 large or 6 small skin-on, boneless chicken thighs

1½ tbsp curry powder

1½ tsp kosher salt

1½ tsp cracked black pepper

1 tbsp extra-virgin olive oil

ASSEMBLY

1 baguette, sliced into 4–6 pieces (depending on the amount of chicken you're using) and split down the middle

A few handfuls of arugula

Sometimes an idea for a sandwich will come to me and I'll think, "That couldn't possibly work." This is one of those sandwiches. The idea started with cinnamon butter. Flavored butter is most definitely a thing, and cinnamon butter is used in sweet applications all the time—but what would happen if I used it in a savory sandwich? It turns out it works beautifully! I made this for some friends at one of my earliest sandwich parties, and it was a hit. When the cinnamon, curry, and cumin come together with the succulent, juicy chicken, fresh tomatoes, and toasty baguette, a truly charming sandwich is born.

A good takeaway from this recipe is the way I cook the chicken— low and slow, in a cast-iron pan over medium-low heat, and finishing with a butter bath. Perfect. There are many ways to cook chicken thighs, but this method guarantees juicy, tender thighs every time. Oh, and don't worry if you have leftover butter—it's great on pancakes and toast and even added to coffee and will store well in the fridge, covered, for up to a month. There is no sauce on this sandwich, so be generous when slathering on that butter.

Start by making the whipped butter. Place the butter, maple syrup, cinnamon, and salt in a mixing bowl. Using a hand mixer, whip until light and fluffy. Set aside.

Next up is the tomato salad. To a mixing bowl add the tomato wedges, shallot, garlic, cumin, salt, and pepper and gently toss. Drizzle in the olive oil and lemon juice and toss again. Cover and refrigerate until ready to use.

Now for the chicken. Place the chicken thighs in a mixing bowl and sprinkle with the curry powder, salt, and pepper. Use your hands to cover the thighs in the spices, ensuring they are well coated.

Heat the oil in a large cast-iron pan over medium-low heat. Let the oil heat up for about 30 seconds, then gently place the coated thighs skin side down into the hot pan. Let the chicken cook in the pan for 10–12 minutes, or until the skin has crisped up. Add 1–2 tbsp of the whipped cinnamon maple butter to the pan and let it melt. Tilt the pan and baste the thighs with the melted butter and pan juices. Continue basting for a minute or so, then flip the thighs. The chicken will have beautiful crispy skin and the meat will be juicy and tender, perfect for a sandwich. Continue to cook for another few minutes, then remove and place on a plate.

CONTINUED

When you're ready to assemble, place half the baguette slices cut side down in the pan the chicken was cooked in. Fry for a few minutes or until golden, slightly crispy, and with a few charred edges. The baguettes will take on all the exquisite flavors from the chicken. Add a bit more of the butter to the pan and repeat with the remaining baguette slices.

To assemble, spread a bit of the whipped butter on the cut sides of the top and bottom baguette slices. Top the bottom slices with some arugula, tomato cumin salad, and chicken thighs, and get ready to fall in love with this sandwich.

NOTE

Skin-on, boneless chicken thighs may not be the easiest thing to find, so here's an easy step-by-step guide to deboning chicken thighs:

1. Lay the thigh skin side down on your cutting board.

2. Using a sharp knife, cut along the length of the bone using a gentle slicing motion, and slide the knife beside the bone to detach the meat.

3. Using your fingers, lift the meat away from the bone and cut any remaining connective tissues.

Practice makes perfect here, once you've done this a few times you'll easily master it.

SUAVE SHORT RIBS

BEEF SHORT RIBS WITH STOUT / HORSERADISH & GRAINY MUSTARD SAUCE / BAGUETTE

MAKES 6 SANDWICHES

SHORT RIBS

6 English-cut beef short ribs

Kosher salt

2 tbsp extra-virgin olive oil

2 red onions, cut into 8 wedges each

4 cloves garlic, minced

1½ tsp ground cinnamon

1½ tsp ground cumin

1½ tsp ground ginger

1½ tsp cayenne

1½ tsp smoked paprika

¼ cup tomato paste

1 tbsp prepared horseradish

1 can Guinness (or your favorite stout)

2 cups beef stock

HORSERADISH & GRAINY MUSTARD SAUCE

½ cup sour cream

1 tbsp creamed horseradish

2 tbsp grainy mustard

1 tbsp Dijon mustard

1 tsp runny honey

½ tsp cracked black pepper

¼ tsp kosher salt

ASSEMBLY

1 baguette, split down the middle and toasted

2 tomatoes, sliced

Some sandwiches come together quickly, while others take a bit longer. Because the ribs in this recipe must hang out in the oven for 2½ hours, you get some time to check a few things off your to-do list. This sandwich could be why you finally organize that drawer everyone has in the kitchen (you know the one, full of everything from last week's takeout menus to random nails, countless cords, and electronics). Use this sandwich to help you organize your life! Or sit back on the couch and read a good book; the choice is yours.

I love horseradish and the pungent, tingling sensation that it delivers, and it appears a few times in this book. If you didn't know, horseradish has been used for hundreds of thousands of years in cooking and medicine. The name we know this root by dates back to England in the late 1500s. Breaking it down, *horse* was meant to symbolize strength and *radish* refers to the type of root it is. I was originally told a very different story about why it has its name, but I'll let you look that one up on your own!

Preheat the oven to 325°F.

Let's start with the short ribs. Liberally season the ribs on all sides with salt. Heat the oil in a large Dutch oven over medium-high heat. Sear the ribs on all sides until a nice crust forms, a few minutes per side.

Remove the short ribs to a plate and add the onions to the Dutch oven. Cook, stirring frequently, until they begin to soften, about 5–6 minutes. Add the garlic, cinnamon, cumin, ginger, cayenne, smoked paprika, tomato paste, and horseradish and stir to combine. Cook for 2 minutes.

Add the stout and beef stock, crank up the heat, bring to a boil, and give the pot a good stir. Turn the heat off, return the ribs to the Dutch oven, cover, and place in the hot oven to braise for 3 hours. Now you have time to prep my chocolate carrot cake on page 228; it would go oh so nicely with this sandwich.

When ready, remove the Dutch oven from the oven and place the meat in a large bowl; the bones will have separated from the meat and you can discard them. Let the meat sit and contemplate its impending fate until slightly cooled, about 20 minutes. Using two forks, shred the meat into beautifully bite-sized pieces.

CONTINUED

Strain the liquid in the Dutch oven, discard the onions and garlic, and skim off most but not all the fat; a little bit of rendered fat will go a long way in helping add flavor to the sauce you're about to make. Yes, you're about to make a sauce, and yes, it's going to be delicious.

Return the liquid to the Dutch oven and place it back on the stove, turn the heat to medium-high, and bring it to a boil. Reduce the heat to medium and simmer until the sauce has thickened and reduced, about 15 minutes or until it comfortably coats the back of a spoon. Ladle some of the sauce over the shredded meat and mix to combine. Add more sauce to the meat until you're happy—the more sauce, the messier.

To make the horseradish sauce, mix the sour cream, horseradish, mustards, honey, pepper, and salt in a bowl.

To assemble, spoon a generous amount of sauced meat onto the bottom half of the baguette, drizzle with some horseradish sauce, add some sliced tomatoes, and close with the top half of the baguette. Slice into individual portions and enjoy!

THE MEATBALL

MEATBALLS / COLLARD GREEN PESTO / MOZZARELLA / ITALIAN ROLL

MAKES 4 SANDWICHES

COLLARD GREEN PESTO

3 cups roughly chopped collard greens (stems removed)

1 cup roughly chopped purple kale (stems removed)

⅓ cup macadamia nuts

2 cloves garlic

1 cup finely grated parmesan

Zest and juice of 1 lemon

½ tsp chili flakes

1 tsp kosher salt

⅓ cup extra-virgin olive oil

MEATBALLS

1 lb (454 g) ground beef

8 oz (225 g) ground pork

1 large egg

⅓ cup packed sun-dried tomatoes, chopped

¼ cup finely grated parmesan

1 tsp kosher salt

½ tsp garlic powder

½ tsp onion powder

1 tsp cracked black pepper

1 tbsp extra-virgin olive oil

ASSEMBLY

4 Italian rolls, partially cut in half

12 slices mozzarella

Chili flakes for garnish (optional)

I could not write a book on sandwiches and not include a meatball sandwich of my own. This one is all about the pesto. It's delicious. I think you'll love it so much you'll want to steal it to use in other dishes. I keep a jar in the fridge to add to pasta when I need a quick meal. It can also be repurposed; just add a little olive oil to a few tablespoons of pesto, and poof!—you've got a tremendous green dressing perfect on a salad or roasted vegetables.

This was one of the earliest recipes I developed for the book, so I have a soft spot for it—sort of like your first child. I made this for my first sandwich party in Toronto, and it was a huge hit. While people tended to have different opinions about most of the other sandwiches I served that night, this one was pretty unanimously voted the fave.

Start by making the pesto. Place the collard greens, kale, macadamia nuts, garlic, parmesan, lemon zest and juice, chili flakes, and salt in a food processor. Blitz for a few seconds to get things moving, then, with the motor running, slowly drizzle in the oil and continue to process until smooth. Set aside.

To make the meatballs, place all the ingredients except the olive oil in a mixing bowl and mix everything with your hands until well combined. The goal is to form 12 equal-ish meatballs—but hey, it's a meatball sandwich, so no need for these balls to be perfect!

Heat the olive oil in a pan over medium-high heat. Add half the meatballs to the pan and sear on all sides. Turn down the heat to medium and continue to cook until the meatballs are cooked through, about 10–15 minutes. If you're wondering if the meatballs are done, an instant-read thermometer inserted into the middle of a fully cooked meatball will read 165°F. Repeat with the remaining meatballs.

Turn the oven to broil and line a baking sheet with foil.

To assemble, spread a generous amount of the pesto onto each roll and nestle three meatballs inside. Top each meatball with a slice of mozzarella, then place on the prepared baking sheet and into the oven for 1 minute or until the cheese is nicely melted and bubbly. Garnish with chili flakes (if using) and enjoy!

THE FEROZ BUN KABAB

ALOO TIKKI / GREEN CHUTNEY / PICKLED RED ONION / BRIOCHE

MAKES 4 SANDWICHES

QUICK PICKLED RED ONION

1 red onion, sliced into thin rounds

1 cup white vinegar

GREEN CHUTNEY

1 bunch fresh cilantro, roughly chopped

½ bunch fresh mint, roughly chopped

½ tsp ground cumin

1 green chile, roughly chopped

½ dried red chile, crushed (optional)

¼ yellow onion, roughly chopped (optional)

Juice of ½ lemon

ALOO TIKKI KABAB

1 tsp cumin seeds

1 tsp coriander seeds

4–5 medium Yukon Gold potatoes, peeled, boiled, mashed, and cooled

½ bunch fresh cilantro, finely chopped

2 green onions, finely minced

1 green chile, finely minced

½ tsp red chili powder

1 tsp kosher salt

2 large eggs

2 cups dried breadcrumbs or panko

¼ cup extra-virgin olive oil

ASSEMBLY

4 brioche buns

1 tsp extra-virgin olive oil

My sister-in-law, Afsah, and her family immigrated to Canada from Pakistan in 1997 and settled in Toronto. Something that was, and still is, ever-present on the streets of Karachi, where they lived, is the bun kebab. Popular all over the country, bun kebabs are sold at fast-food restaurants and by street-cart vendors and eaten as a late-night snack or a hearty dinner. Although native to Pakistan, the bun kebab is now widely eaten throughout the Indian subcontinent and all over the world. There are many varieties composed of meat, lentils, or potatoes. We're going vegetarian here and using potatoes as the star ingredient. The recipe you're about to make is borrowed directly from Afsah's parents. Her mother, Fauzia, contributed the aloo tikki recipe (*aloo* meaning "potato" and *tikki* meaning "small cutlet" or "croquette"), and her father, Tariq, contributed the green chutney recipe. It's a family affair, and I hope you enjoy this sandwich as much as I do.

First up is the quick pickled red onion. In a bowl, combine the onion slices and vinegar and let sit for 30 minutes. They'll be crunchy and vinegary by the time you're ready to assemble the sandwiches.

Next up is the green chutney. Place the cilantro, mint, cumin, green chile, and red chile and onion (if using) in a food processor and process on high until a chunky chutney has been achieved. Set aside.

And now we make the aloo tikki. Start by toasting the spices. In a small dry frying pan set over medium-high heat, toast the cumin and coriander seeds, swirling the pan every so often, for about 3–4 minutes. The seeds will darken in color and release a beautiful fragrant aroma. Use a coffee grinder or mortar and pestle to grind the toasted seeds into a powder.

Transfer the cumin and coriander powder to a large mixing bowl and add the mashed potatoes, cilantro, green onions, green chile, chili powder, and salt. Mix well to combine. Wet your hands slightly before forming the potato mixture into four patties.

Set up your breading stations. Crack the eggs into one bowl and whisk. Place the breadcrumbs in another bowl. Heat the oil in a large frying pan over medium-high heat. Line a baking sheet with paper towels and place a wire rack on top.

Dip the patties first into the eggs, then carefully into the breadcrumbs to coat. Working in batches as needed, fry for about 2–3 minutes per side or until nicely golden brown. Remove and place on the wire rack.

Once all the kababs have been fried, fry the inside and outside of each bun in the same pan, adding a little more oil if needed and ensuring you get some nice color on the outside top bun.

To assemble, spread a good amount of the chutney onto the bottom bun, then top with kabab and some pickled red onion. Close the sandwich with the toasted top bun and enjoy!

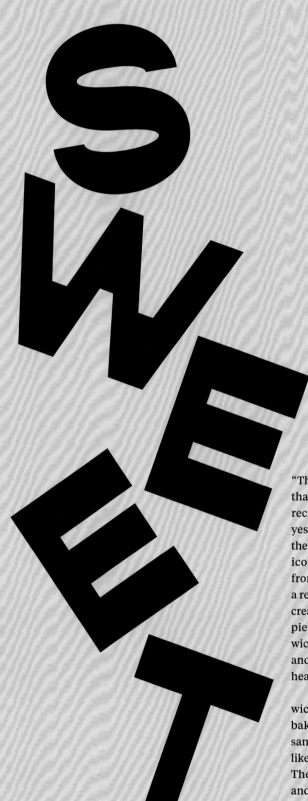

"There are sweet sandwiches in the book?" I got that question a lot when writing and testing out recipes. My answer was always the same: "Hell, yes!" There was never a doubt in my mind that there would be a sweet chapter. There are so many iconic sweet sandwiches out there to choose from, like classic French macarons (yup, I've got a recipe for those in here), the always famous ice cream sandwich (there are two), and the whoopie pie (one of those). Throw in a few cookie sand-wiches and a few other sweet and delicious treats, and you'll be baking your way to sweet sandwich heaven before you know it.

For most of my recipes, save for the few sand-wiches with their own bread recipe, there is little baking to do—until now, that is. But fear not, sandwich lovers! If you're not a baker, or you feel like baking might not be your thing, do not worry! The recipes in this chapter are straightforward and will have you dancing in your kitchen in no time—I promise!

A Really Chocolaty Sandwich

BROWNIE COOKIE / SALTED CARAMEL GANACHE

MAKES 6 SANDWICHES

BROWNIE COOKIES

1 cup finely chopped dark chocolate

½ cup unsalted butter, cubed

1 tsp vanilla extract

2 large eggs

¾ cup granulated sugar

½ cup brown sugar, packed

1 tsp kosher salt

¾ cup all-purpose flour

½ cup cocoa powder

Flaky salt

SALTED CARAMEL GANACHE

⅓ cup granulated sugar

1 tbsp water

½ cup heavy cream

1 tsp flaky salt

1 cup finely chopped milk chocolate

Be warned, friends, this sweet sandwich is decadent! It's the perfect sandwich to share with your love or your best friend—or, heck, if you love chocolate, have the whole damn thing yourself! Like any good brownie, the cookies are fudgy, chewy, and a chocolate lover's dream.

As with all the sweet sandwiches in the book, there are at least two elements to make to get to the sandwich. The great thing is that most of these elements can be made and enjoyed separately if you wish. Spread this ganache on a cake or use it as a sweet spread on toast on a rainy Sunday morning. The brownie cookies can be made in advance, stored at room temperature in an airtight container for up to 4 days, and frozen for up to 3 months. But let's be honest, who's going to do that?

We'll start with the cookies. Position a rack in the center of the oven, preheat the oven to 350°F, and line two baking sheets with parchment paper.

Place the chopped chocolate and butter in a double boiler (a metal or glass mixing bowl placed over a saucepan filled with 2 inches of simmering water). Let the heat from the steam slowly melt the chocolate and butter. Begin to stir once pools of chocolate and butter start to form. Once fully melted and incorporated, remove from the heat, add the vanilla, stir to combine, and set aside.

Place the eggs, sugars, and kosher salt in the bowl of a stand mixer fitted with the whisk attachment (alternatively, you can use a large mixing bowl and a hand mixer). Whisk on high for 5 minutes; the mixture will have thickened and turned pale yellow. Turn the speed to low, slowly and carefully pour in the chocolate mixture, and continue to mix until fully incorporated.

Remove the bowl from the stand mixer and sift in the flour and cocoa powder. Gently mix until no flour streaks remain, but be careful not to overmix the batter.

Use a ¼-cup measuring cup or small ice cream scoop to scoop the batter onto the prepared baking sheets, placing 6 evenly spaced scoops on each sheet. This can become a bit messy, but don't worry, in baking every good mess delivers a delicious payoff, I promise! Get in there and use your fingers to draw every last bit of batter out of the measuring cup (and go ahead and lick them once you're done).

CONTINUED

209

Bake, one tray at a time, for 10 minutes. Remove the cookies from the oven and quickly slam the baking sheet onto the counter—this helps the cookies develop their signature brownie cracks. Return to the oven to finish baking for 2 minutes. Remove from the oven and immediately sprinkle the cookies with flaky salt. Let them cool completely on the baking sheets.

While the cookies cool, make the ganache. In a small saucepan over medium heat, combine the sugar and water and mix until the sugar is moistened. Let the mixture cook, swirling the pan every so often, for about 5 minutes or until the caramel has turned a nice toasty brown. Slowly and gently whisk in the cream and salt until fully incorporated and smooth. Remove from heat.

Place the milk chocolate in a medium mixing bowl and pour the hot caramel overtop. Let sit for 5 minutes. Whisk the caramel into the melted chocolate until smooth and incorporated, then place the bowl in the fridge to set for 1 hour.

To assemble, dollop a heaping tablespoon of the ganache onto the flat sides of half of the brownie cookies and sandwich the remaining cookies on top. Enjoy!

SALT

Probably not the first word you'd expect to read in a sweet sandwich recipe, but stay with me, friends. Sodium chloride, better known as salt (it's made up of about 60% chloride and 40% sodium) is possibly the biggest workhorse in your pantry (if not the biggest) and is used in both savory and sweet dishes.

Why does salt work so exquisitely when paired with these sweet desserts? Let me explain. When salt is used in baking, whether in caramel or chocolate desserts or even on the tops of my brownie cookies and throughout this chapter, salt is essentially waking up your taste buds to the presence of sugar, sending a message directly to the brain that says, "Hey, brain, you're about to eat something sweet—pay attention!" We know there are five basic taste receptor cells on the tongue: bitter, sweet, salty, sour, and umami, and when salt hits these receptors, it helps balance out flavor, enhance sweetness, and, most importantly, neutralize bitterness. In short, the addition of salt, whether it is within the main ingredients or used as a finisher, strengthens, enhances, and sharpens these recipes, and let me tell you, your taste buds will cheer.

Salted caramel is everywhere these days, from lattes and chocolates to cookies and cakes. Walk the aisles of your local Walmart and you'll see it from here to Sunday, from salted caramel vodka to peanut butter and yogurt, and even candles and bath bombs. It was in 1977 in the region of Brittany, in France's most famous salt marshes, that the French chef Henri Le Roux is credited with first creating this most unique, delectable, and now ubiquitous flavor combination. Le Roux, a chocolatier, wanted to be able to highlight Brittany's most prominent export—its salted butter, or *beurre salé*. After a few years of testing, he brilliantly developed the recipe for *caramels au beurre salé*, or "salted butter caramels," and within a few years, it was recognized as *le meilleur bonbon de France*, "best candy in France," at the Salon international de la confiserie in Paris. This was in 1980, and now, decades later, it has become one of the culinary world's most loved flavor combinations.

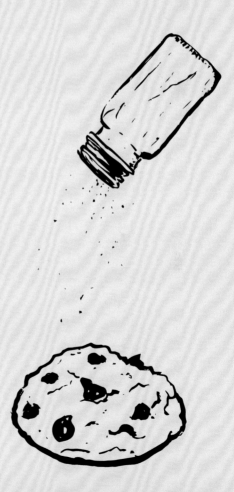

Crème Brûlée
Cookie Sandwich

BROWN BUTTER SUGAR COOKIE / CUSTARD / CREAM CHEESE

MAKES 9 SANDWICHES

COOKIES

1 cup unsalted butter, cubed

2 cups all-purpose flour

1 tsp baking soda

1 tsp cornstarch

1 tsp kosher salt

1 cup dark brown sugar, packed

½ cup granulated sugar

2 large eggs

2 tsp vanilla extract

CUSTARD

1 cup unsalted butter, softened

1 cup icing sugar

¼ cup custard powder

¼ cup heavy cream

1 tsp vanilla bean paste (or vanilla extract)

½ tsp kosher salt

TOPPING

9 oz (250 g) cream cheese

1 cup icing sugar

1 tsp vanilla extract

¼ tsp kosher salt

⅓ cup superfine sugar

I really wanted a crème brûlée sandwich in this book; I just could not figure out how that would look. Ask my friend Sonia, pastry chef and recipe tester extraordinaire, how long I tried to figure this one out. It started out very different from what you see here, with a bun instead of a cookie and a much more complicated custard. It was one of those recipes I kept changing and returning to weekly, but that's the joy of recipe testing, and I think I landed on a great one. It is not too difficult and will give you a bit of a wow factor when you serve it at your next dinner party or bring it to that yearly cookie exchange. If you've always wanted to make crème brûlée but were afraid to try (or did not want to do all the work), these little guys are for you.

Let's start with the cookies, and for that we'll need to brown some butter. Place the butter in a medium sauté pan over medium heat and let it melt. Swirl the pan frequently to prevent the butter from burning. Cook until it browns and smells beautifully nutty, about 5–7 minutes. Remove the pan from the heat and immediately transfer the butter to a large mixing bowl. Let cool slightly.

In a medium mixing bowl, whisk together the flour, baking soda, cornstarch, and salt. Set aside.

Once the brown butter has cooled, add both the sugars and whisk until combined. Add the eggs and vanilla and continue to whisk until fully incorporated and smooth.

Slowly add the flour mixture to the wet ingredients, switch to a silicone spatula or wooden spoon, and mix until well combined. Wrap the dough with plastic wrap and chill in the fridge for at least 2 hours.

Place a rack in the center of the oven, preheat the oven to 350°F, and line two baking sheets with parchment paper.

Portion the dough using a 2½ tbsp scoop and place 6 balls of dough on each baking sheet, spaced evenly, as the cookies will spread when baked (you're making 18 cookies in total so don't use up all of the dough yet). Bake, one tray at a time, until nicely golden brown around the edges, about 12–14 minutes. Remove from the oven and let cool for 5 minutes on the baking sheet, then transfer to a wire rack to cool completely. Repeat with the remaining dough to make the final 6 cookies.

CONTINUED

213

Next up, we'll tackle the custard filling. Using a stand mixer fitted with the paddle attachment or a medium bowl and a hand mixer, beat the butter on high until smooth and creamy. Turn the mixer off, scrape down the sides of the bowl, and add the icing sugar. Turn the speed to low and let the mixture slowly incorporate. After about a minute, turn the speed to medium and beat until fully incorporated. Add the custard powder, cream, vanilla, and salt, slowly turn the speed up to high, and beat until fluffy. Transfer the custard to a clean bowl, cover and refrigerate for 30 minutes to firm up. Clean the bowl of the stand mixer before making the topping.

For the topping, place the cream cheese in the bowl of the stand mixer and beat on high until smooth. Turn the speed down to low, carefully add the icing sugar, and beat until fully incorporated. Turn the speed up to high and beat in the vanilla and salt.

Before assembling these sandwiches, you're going to create the brûlée tops. Add the superfine sugar to a plate. Gently spread about a tablespoon of the cream cheese topping to on the tops of half the cookies. Carefully dip them into the plate of sugar, coating the cream cheese topping with sugar. Use a kitchen torch to caramelize the sugared topping.

To assemble, dollop a tablespoon of the custard on the bottoms of the remaining cookies. Finish by placing the brûléed cookies on top of the custard and gingerly pressing them together. Enjoy!

Jumbo Lemon Honey Macarons

LEMON CURD / HONEY / CREAM CHEESE / BEE POLLEN

MAKES 12 SANDWICHES

COOKIES

1¾ cups finely ground almond flour

2 cups icing sugar

½ tsp kosher salt

4 large egg whites, room temperature

¼ tsp cream of tartar

½ cup superfine sugar

5 drops yellow food coloring gel

½ tsp lemon extract

2 tbsp bee pollen, ground (see note)

LEMON CURD

2 large eggs, room temperature

¼ cup runny honey

Zest and juice of 2 lemons

3 tbsp unsalted butter, cubed

FILLING

2 tbsp unsalted butter, softened

⅓ cup cream cheese, softened

2 tbsp runny honey

Zest of 1 lemon

3 cups icing sugar

RECIPE PHOTO ON PAGE 218

Although chocolate is a strong contender in the race for the most loved dessert ingredient, I would venture to say the mighty lemon is right on its heels. There is something so satisfying about a lemon dessert after dinner. Usually not too sweet, with punches of tartness, the lemon is confident in its tang. Like chocolate, it can carry the whole thing like a prominent Hollywood actor can carry a film. Okay, that's a bit of a stretch, but you get what I'm saying—the lemon is a star!

I wanted to include a macaron recipe in this book because it is the perfect example of a sweet sandwich. If you've never made them before, they might seem intimidating—especially if you've ever had them from a beautiful display in a French patisserie. But trust me, making your own at home is easier than you might think. Once you've mastered them, you'll be coming up with your own flavor combinations before you know it!

We're starting this recipe with the cookies. In a food processor, pulse the almond flour, powdered sugar, and salt together until well combined and finely ground. Sift the mixture into a large mixing bowl, and then sift once more to ensure the smoothest texture in the baked cookies. Discard any pieces left in the sieve.

Place the egg whites in the bowl of a stand mixer fitted with the whisk attachment, or use a hand mixer and a large mixing bowl. Whisk on low until they become foamy, about 1 minute, then add the cream of tartar. Turn the speed to medium and continue whisking for another minute. With the mixer running slowly, add the sugar. Once all the sugar is added, turn up the speed to high, add the yellow food coloring and continue to whisk until stiff peaks form, about 4–5 minutes. Gently fold in the lemon extract.

Confidently fold in about a third of the dry almond flour mixture to the whipped egg whites, until combined. Add the rest of the almond flour mixture and gently fold until combined, but do not overmix; you're looking for a smooth and viscous batter.

Line two baking sheets with parchment paper. Add the batter to a piping bag fitted with a large round tip. Pipe 3-inch circles of batter onto the prepared baking sheets, about 1 inch apart (you want 24 in total, 12 on each sheet). Tap the baking sheet against the counter a few times to release any air bubbles. Sprinkle the cookies with the

CONTINUED

215

ground bee pollen, then let them air-dry for 1½ hours. You know they're ready to bake when you can run your finger across the top of the cookies and they feel dry and no longer tacky.

Position a rack in the center of the oven and preheat the oven to 300°F.

Bake the macarons for 20 minutes, one tray at a time, rotating them halfway through baking. When they come out of the oven they will have developed ruffled and slightly raised edges (or feet as they are known), and easily lift from the baking sheets. Let the macarons cool completely on the baking sheets.

While the cookies cool, we can make the curd and the filling. First up is the curd. Place the eggs and honey in a medium saucepan and whisk until thoroughly combined. Add the lemon zest and juice and continue whisking. Place the saucepan over medium heat and continue whisking for about 6–8 minutes or until thickened enough to coat the back of a wooden spoon. Remove from the heat and add the butter. Whisk until the butter has melted and is fully incorporated.

Strain the curd through a fine-mesh sieve set over a medium mixing bowl, using a silicone spatula to coax all the curd through the sieve. Set aside to cool completely.

And finally, the cream cheese filling. Place the butter, cream cheese, honey, and lemon zest in the bowl of a stand mixer fitted with the paddle attachment, or use a hand mixer and medium mixing bowl. Mix on medium-high speed until fluffy, about 3–4 minutes. Turn the mixer off and add half the icing sugar. Slowly turn the mixer back to low speed and mix to incorporate. Repeat with remaining icing sugar. Turn the mixer to high and whip to combine thoroughly.

To assemble the macarons, spoon the cream cheese filling into a piping bag fitted with the tip of your choosing. Pipe a circle of filling on the flat sides of half of the cookies and dollop some cooled curd into the middle of each circle. Sandwich with the remaining cookies on top. Enjoy!

NOTE Bee pollen might be hard to find, but don't stress. If you can't find it these macarons will be just as delicious without.

Strawberry Confetti Ice Cream Sandwich

STRAWBERRY CONFETTI ICE CREAM / CONFETTI COOKIE

MAKES 16 SANDWICHES

STRAWBERRY CONFETTI ICE CREAM

4 pints strawberry ice cream

2 cups confetti sprinkles

CONFETTI COOKIES

1 cup unsalted butter, room temperature

1 cup granulated sugar

½ cup brown sugar, packed

2 large eggs

1½ tsp vanilla extract

2¼ cups all-purpose flour

2 tsp cornstarch

1 tsp baking soda

½ tsp kosher salt

1 cup confetti sprinkles

RECIPE PHOTO ON PAGE 206

Simple, fun, and perfect for summer. This one is for the kids—or the adults who want to pretend they're still kids!

We'll start with the ice cream. Place it in a large mixing bowl and let it soften slightly (do not throw out the containers). Scatter the sprinkles all over the ice cream and mix them in, using a rubber spatula so they are evenly distributed. Return the ice cream to the original containers and place them back in the freezer to refreeze.

To make the confetti cookies, in the bowl of a stand mixer fitted with the paddle attachment, or using a hand mixer, beat the butter and sugars together until nicely combined, about 3 minutes. Scrape down the sides of the bowl, add the eggs and vanilla, and continue to beat until fully incorporated, about 1 minute.

Whisk together the flour, cornstarch, baking soda, and salt in a medium mixing bowl.

Add the flour mixture to the butter mixture and mix until well combined. Fold in the sprinkles. Cover the dough with plastic wrap and refrigerate for 2 hours.

Position a rack in the top and bottom thirds of the oven, preheat the oven to 350°F, and line two baking sheets with parchment paper.

Portion the dough using a 2 tbsp scoop. Place 8 balls of dough on each baking sheet, spaced evenly, as the cookies will spread when baked (you're making 32 cookies in total so only use half the dough just now). Bake, two trays at a time (rotating and switching the position of the trays in the oven halfway through), until the edges of the cookies are beautifully golden and their centers proudly puffed, about 10–12 minutes. Let the cookies cool for 5 minutes on the baking sheet, then transfer to a wire rack to cool completely. Repeat with the remaining dough, to make the remaining 16 cookies.

To make the sandwiches, scoop a generous amount of strawberry confetti ice cream onto half of the cookies and sandwich the remaining cookies on top. Enjoy!

My Favorite Ice Cream Sandwich

GINGER & OLIVE OIL COOKIE / PEACH & GINGER ICE CREAM

MAKES 15 SANDWICHES

NO-CHURN PEACH & GINGER ICE CREAM

4 peaches, peeled and chopped into 1-inch pieces

¼ cup granulated sugar

1 tsp lemon juice

1 (10 fl oz/300 mL) can sweetened condensed milk

1 tbsp vanilla extract

¼ cup brown sugar, packed

2 cups heavy cream

⅓ cup crystallized ginger, finely chopped

GINGER & OLIVE OIL COOKIES

2½ cups dark brown sugar, packed

2 cups extra-virgin olive oil

½ cup fancy molasses

2 large eggs

4 cups all-purpose flour

4 tsp baking soda

1½ tsp kosher salt

1 tbsp ground ginger

1½ tsp ground cinnamon

1 tsp ground allspice

½ cup granulated sugar

RECIPE PHOTO ON PAGE 222

In my humble opinion, the trick to a good ice cream sandwich is for the cookie to be soft and chewy. A crisp or flaky cookie will prevent you from getting a bite with that perfect cookie–to–ice cream ratio. But a soft, chewy cookie will allow you to successfully bite into the sandwich without all the ice cream falling out the sides.

These cookies are not only soft and chewy but rich with a bit of spice from the ginger, cinnamon, and allspice, and a perfect partner for peach and ginger ice cream. The ice cream is sweet with a kick from the crystallized ginger. These sandwiches are a summer treat that could easily be eaten into the fall, and why not make them at Christmastime and surprise your family and friends? Pretend you're celebrating Christmas in July. I originally developed this recipe for a Christmas-in-July segment I did way back in 2019 for *CTV Your Morning*. I've adapted it a bit along the way, adding the olive oil to the cookie for richness. I hope you enjoy these all year round, because I love them so much!

For the no-churn ice cream, begin with the peaches. Place the chopped peaches, sugar, and lemon juice in a medium pot over medium-high heat and mix to combine. Let the mixture come to a boil, then reduce the heat to medium-low and simmer for about 15–20 minutes, stirring every 30 seconds or so to prevent the peaches from sticking. Remove from the heat and let cool completely.

In a large bowl, whisk together the sweetened condensed milk and vanilla. Add the cooled stewed peaches and brown sugar and gently fold until combined.

In the bowl of a stand mixer fitted with the whisk attachment or in a bowl using a hand mixer, beat the cream until stiff peaks form. Delicately fold the whipped cream into the peach mixture, then fold in the ginger.

Pour the mixture into a 5 × 9-inch loaf pan, wrap in plastic wrap, and freeze overnight.

Now it's time to make the cookie dough. Place the brown sugar, olive oil, molasses, and eggs in a large bowl and whisk until fully incorporated and the mixture resembles a dark, loose caramel.

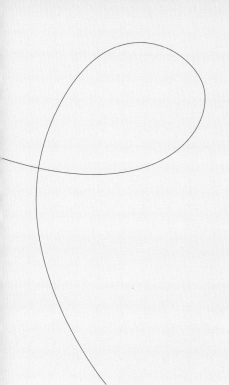

Place the flour, baking soda, salt, ginger, cinnamon, and allspice in a separate mixing bowl. Whisk until combined. Slowly add the dry ingredients to the wet, mixing until all the dry ingredients have been incorporated to form a dough. Cover and chill the dough for 2–3 hours.

Position a rack in the center of the oven and preheat to 375°F. Line two baking sheets with parchment paper and add the granulated sugar to a bowl.

Portion the dough using a 2½ tbsp scoop into 30 balls of dough and roll each ball in granulated sugar. Place 6 balls of dough on each baking sheet, spaced evenly, as the cookies will spread when baked. Bake, one tray at a time, until the edges are golden and slightly crisp, the centers wonderfully soft, and the tops delightfully crinkly, about 12–14 minutes. Let the cookies cool for 5 minutes on the baking sheet, then transfer to a wire rack to cool completely. Repeat with the remaining dough balls to bake a total of 30 cookies.

To assemble one sandwich, place a scoop of ice cream on one of the cookies, sandwich with another cookie, and gently press down. Enjoy!

(NO OFFENSE, STRAWBERRY ICE CREAM SANDWICH, I LOVE YOU TOO!)

Sonia Saves the Day: 1 Cookie, 3 Fillings

DARK CHOCOLATE COOKIE / PEANUT BUTTER BOURBON / RASPBERRY CREAM CHEESE / BURNT MARSHMALLOW

MAKES 15 SANDWICHES

DARK CHOCOLATE COOKIES

2 cups all-purpose flour

6 tbsp cocoa powder

1 tbsp espresso powder

1 tsp baking soda

1 tsp kosher salt

1 cup unsalted butter, melted

2 large eggs

½ cup granulated sugar

1½ cups brown sugar, packed

2 tsp vanilla extract

1½ cups chopped dark chocolate

Flaky salt

PEANUT BUTTER BOURBON FILLING

4½ oz (125 g) cream cheese, softened

¼ cup crunchy or smooth peanut butter

2 tbsp unsalted butter, softened

1 tbsp bourbon

1 tsp vanilla extract

1½ cups icing sugar

RASPBERRY CREAM CHEESE FILLING

1 cup fresh raspberries

2 tbsp granulated sugar

1 (9 oz/250 g) package cream cheese, softened

½ tsp vanilla extract

MARSHMALLOW FILLING

4 large egg whites, at room temperature

¾ cup granulated sugar

¼ tsp cream of tartar

1 tsp vanilla extract

RECIPE PHOTO ON PAGE 226

I love this recipe because it's a sort of choose-your-own-adventure type of recipe. A dark chocolate cookie is the base for all three options, and there are three fillings to choose from—all very different and all very delicious. First, we have the peanut butter bourbon filling. Peanut butter and dark chocolate are old lovers and will always have a place in their hearts for each other. Add bourbon to the mix and you're asking for trouble! Just kidding, it's a great addition, but if you're not into booze, feel free to leave it out.

The raspberry cream cheese filling was a bit of a fluke. When we were shooting the cookbook, I initially had a pumpkin and rum filling instead of this one. But when we put the pumpkin-filled cookie sandwiches next to the peanut butter–filled ones, they were virtually identical, and I knew I needed to make a quick change. Enter my friend Sonia, who was on set helping out that day. With raspberries and cream cheese in hand, she saved the day with filling number two. Simple, but a perfect pairing with these dark chocolate cookies.

Last but not least, the burnt marshmallow. So pretty to have after dinner or at a cookie exchange; serve this version open-faced so everyone can see your beautiful work, or throw another cookie on top to make a proper cookie sandwich. Either way, they are sure to be a hit.

First, let's make the dark chocolate cookies. Place the flour, cocoa powder, espresso powder, baking soda, and salt in a mixing bowl. Whisk until well combined and set aside.

In another mixing bowl, whisk to combine the melted butter, eggs, sugars, and vanilla. Switching to a silicone spatula or a wooden spoon, slowly add the dry ingredients to the wet ingredients, and mix until fully incorporated and no flour streaks remain. Fold in the chopped chocolate. Cover and chill the dough in the fridge for 1 hour.

Position a rack in the center of the oven, preheat the oven to 350°F, and line two baking sheets with parchment paper.

Portion the dough using a 2 tbsp scoop and placing 6 balls of dough on each baking sheet, spaced evenly, as the cookies will spread when baked. Bake, one tray at a time, until the cookies have developed exquisitely crackled tops, about 12 minutes. Remove from the oven and immediately sprinkle with flaky salt and let cool on the baking sheet for 5 minutes, then transfer to a wire rack to cool completely. Repeat with the remaining dough.

While the cookies are cooling, you can make the filling—or fillings, if you're feeling adventurous and decide to make more than one.

For the peanut butter bourbon filling, place all the ingredients except the icing sugar in a large bowl and, using a hand mixer, mix to incorporate. Slowly add the icing sugar, ½ cup at a time, until everything is smooth. Cover and refrigerate until needed.

For the raspberry filling, place the raspberries and sugar in a food processor and pulse until the berries have broken down and released all of their juices. Add the softened cream cheese and vanilla and process until smooth. Set aside.

For the marshmallow filling, place all the ingredients in a metal or glass mixing bowl fitted over a saucepan filled with a few inches of simmering water. While whisking, heat until warm to the touch and the sugar has dissolved, about 3–4 minutes. Remove from the heat and transfer to the bowl of a stand mixer fitted with the whisk attachment, or you can use a mixing bowl and hand mixer. Start at low speed and gradually increase it to high until you have glossy, thick, meringue-like marshmallow.

Once the cookies have cooled and you have the fillings ready, it's time to make the sandwiches. To assemble the peanut butter bourbon and the raspberry cream cheese options, smear 1–2 tbsp of filling onto half the cookies and sandwich with the remaining cookies on top. For the marshmallow filling, spread 1–2 tbsp of filling onto half of the cookies and then quickly torch the topping, using a kitchen torch. Sandwich the remaining cookies on top. Enjoy!

This One Is for You, Mom

CHOCOLATE CARROT CAKE / MASCARPONE CREAM CHEESE

MAKES 8 SANDWICHES

CHOCOLATE CARROT CAKE

½ cup + 2 tbsp unsalted butter

2 cups all-purpose flour

1 tsp baking soda

1 tsp ground cinnamon

1 tsp kosher salt

¼ tsp ground cloves

2 large eggs

1 cup dark brown sugar, packed

1 tsp vanilla extract

½ cup Greek yogurt or any thick yogurt

1½ cups grated carrots

1 cup chopped dark chocolate

MASCARPONE CREAM CHEESE

½ cup mascarpone, softened

½ cup cream cheese, softened

2 tbsp icing sugar

1 tsp vanilla extract

¼ tsp kosher salt

This recipe holds a significant place in my heart. You see, my mom would make my twin brother, Ryan, and me carrot cake every year for our birthdays when we were kids. It wasn't the cake either of us wanted at the time (come on, carrot cake for your 10th birthday?! Where was our chocolate cake, like every other kid on the block?), but it was delicious. She would make each of us our own cake and we'd have leftovers for a week. My mom was an early adopter of the health food movement, having started her journey when she was pregnant with us. Her tattered copy of *Diet for a Small Planet*, initially published in 1971, sat on the kitchen counter, and she would cook from it often. She became so interested in health food and helping others understand how to eat healthier that she eventually opened her own health food store in the early '90s. She called it The Healthy Nuts, which, come on, is a pretty great name for a health food store.

This sandwich is dedicated to her. The cake recipe is hers, but with a few changes. I added the chocolate we wanted when we were kids and I know if I could make it for her today, she would love it.

Position a rack in the center of the oven and preheat the oven to 350°F. Spray a 5 × 9-inch loaf pan with cooking spray and line it with parchment paper.

First, we'll brown the butter. Place the butter in a medium sauté pan over medium heat and let it melt. Swirl the pan frequently to prevent it from burning. Cook until the butter browns and smells pleasantly nutty, about 5–7 minutes. Remove the pan from the heat and immediately transfer the butter to a mixing bowl to cool completely.

In a large bowl, whisk together the flour, baking soda, cinnamon, salt, and cloves.

In another bowl, whisk together the cooled brown butter, eggs, brown sugar, and vanilla until fully incorporated, then whisk in the yogurt.

Pour the wet ingredients into the flour mixture and gently mix until combined. Fold in the carrots and chocolate.

Scrape the batter into the prepared loaf pan and spread it out evenly. Bake for 45–50 minutes or until a toothpick inserted in the middle of the loaf comes out clean. Let the loaf cool in the pan for a few minutes, then remove and place on a wire rack to cool completely.

For the filling, place the mascarpone, cream cheese, icing sugar, and vanilla in a mixing bowl and mix well. I find a silicone spatula works well here.

Once the carrot cake is cool, slice the loaf into 8 equal slices. Slather half the slices with a generous amount of the filling. Top with the remaining slices and cut the sandwiches into triangles. Enjoy!

Chocolate Cherry Whoopie Pies

DARK CHOCOLATE / CHERRY / WHIPPED CREAM

MAKES 6 SANDWICHES

CHOCOLATE CAKES

2 cups all-purpose flour

½ cup cocoa powder

1½ tsp baking soda

½ tsp baking powder

½ tsp kosher salt

½ cup unsalted butter, softened

½ cup dark brown sugar, packed

½ cup granulated sugar

1 large egg

1 tsp vanilla extract

1 cup buttermilk, room temperature

FILLING

1 cup heavy cream

1 tbsp granulated sugar

1 tsp vanilla extract

ASSEMBLY

¼ cup Kirsch (optional)

1 cup cherry jam

⅓ cup finely chopped dark chocolate

Black Forest cake seemed to make an appearance at our house now and then growing up. The bakery my dad frequented, a Slovenian spot that made the rye bread we had every morning and the desserts we got after church on Sunday, also made Black Forest cake. And on special occasions, one of those cakes would make its way home with Dad, and we would devour it, usually in one sitting.

Some say the name of the cake comes from the traditional headdress worn by women from the Black Forest villages in south-western Germany. Called a *bollenhut*, it is adorned with red woolen pompoms and a white brim, hence the cherries and whipped cream that make this cake so iconic. And the chocolate, let's not forget about the chocolate. Layers of chocolate sponge and lots of chocolate shavings make this a chocolate lover's dream.

First we'll make the chocolate cakes. Position a rack in the center of the oven, preheat the oven to 350°F, and line two baking sheets with parchment paper.

In a large mixing bowl, sift together the flour, cocoa powder, baking soda, baking powder, and salt. Set aside.

In the bowl of a stand mixer fitted with the paddle attachment, beat the butter and sugars until light and fluffy, about 3–4 minutes. Beat in the egg and vanilla extract until fully incorporated.

Reduce the mixer speed to low, carefully add half the dry ingredients, and beat for 30 seconds. Scrape down the sides of the bowl if needed. Add half the buttermilk and continue to beat. Repeat these steps until all of the dry ingredients and buttermilk have been added and everything is well combined.

Drop 6 scoops of the batter (about 2 tbsp each) onto each of the prepared baking sheets about 2 inches apart. Bake, one tray at a time, for 10 minutes or until the cakes are firm to the touch and a toothpick inserted into the center comes out clean. Remove from the oven and let cool for 5 minutes on the baking sheet, then transfer to a wire rack to cool completely.

While the cakes cool, you can make the whipped cream filling. Place the cream, sugar, and vanilla in the bowl of a stand mixer fitted with the whisk attachment or use a mixing bowl and a hand mixer; beat the cream on medium-high until stiff peaks form.

CONTINUED

To assemble, generously brush the flat side of each cake with Kirsch. Pipe or spread whipped cream in a ring around the outside edge of half the cookies, leaving an empty circle in the middle. Place a dollop of cherry jam in the middle of each circle and sandwich with the flat side of the remaining cakes on top. Carefully sprinkle the outside edges of whipped cream with a bit of chopped chocolate, and enjoy!

Pure Joy

NECTARINE / APRICOT / SABAYON / PISTACHIO / SWEET BUN

MAKES 8 SANDWICHES

SWEET BUNS

½ cup lukewarm whole milk

2¼ tsp instant yeast (one ¼ oz/8 g packet)

2½ cups bread flour

¼ cup granulated sugar

¼ cup dulce de leche

¼ cup unsalted butter, softened

1 large egg, room temperature

1 tsp kosher salt

1 large egg yolk + 1 tbsp whole milk, whisked

1 tbsp unsalted butter, melted

NECTARINES & APRICOTS

2 ripe nectarines, sliced

3 ripe apricots, sliced

3 tbsp champagne vinegar

3 tbsp granulated sugar

SABAYON

6 large egg yolks

⅓ cup granulated sugar

½ cup Marsala wine

Zest of 1 lemon

ASSEMBLY

½ cup pistachios, finely chopped

There are a few sandwiches in this book that feel like they might be able to play a dual role; that is, they could easily appear in more than one chapter without feeling out of place. This is one of those sandwiches. Although this beauty appears in the Sweet chapter, it could easily hang with the Breakfast crowd down the street.

This recipe was initially developed with peaches, but because I already had a peach recipe, I felt I needed to highlight a different fruit. Luckily for me, my photographer Séb and I shot this book in his parents' beautiful kitchen in Toronto, and his mother, Catherine, who sells her fruit simple syrup at the farmers' market, was able to get me a generous amount of fresh Ontario nectarines and apricots. They worked out beautifully, maybe even better than the peaches. If you have only one of the two fruits, feel free to use it on its own, but the combination of the two really hits.

This is one of the few recipes in the book that require you to bake the bread portion of the sandwich. You can substitute the sweet buns with brioche buns, which will still be delicious, but the buns are easy to make and I think they make for a great sandwich. The bun recipe is loosely based on an Eastern European sweet bun called *buchteln* or *buhteljni* in Slovenian. It can be found in bakeries in Slovenia—where I got to try them on a trip I took with my dad for my 30th birthday—but also in neighboring Austria and Germany. For my version, I've added a bit of dulce de leche. It gives the buns a deep richness that works well with the bright fruit and the punchy sabayon. I hope you enjoy them!

We begin by making the sweet buns. Place the milk, yeast, flour, sugar, dulce de leche, butter, egg, and salt in the bowl of a stand mixer fitted with the paddle attachment. Mix on medium speed until everything comes together, about 1 minute. Switch to the dough hook and knead on medium-high for 12 minutes (let the machine do all the work). The dough will be sticky but soft. Lightly oil a large mixing bowl and place the dough ball in the bowl. Cover with a damp tea towel and let rise for 2 hours, or until doubled in size.

Turn the dough onto a work surface and divide it into eight equal pieces. Shape the dough into balls as best you can, then roll the balls on the work surface with the palm of your hand to smooth them out.

CONTINUED

233

Generously grease an 8-inch round cake pan and place the dough balls into the pan. Cover with a damp tea towel and let the dough proof for about an hour.

Preheat the oven to 350°F.

Lightly brush the tops of the buns with the egg yolk and milk mixture. Bake for 28–30 minutes; they are done when an instant-read thermometer reads 190°F when inserted into one of the buns.

Remove from the oven and brush the tops with melted butter. Place the pan on a wire rack to cool for 20 minutes. Run a butter knife around the edge of the pan to release the buns onto the wire rack, and continue to cool. Once cooled, slice the buns in half in preparation for sandwich making.

While the buns cool, you can take care of the nectarines and apricots. Place the fruit in a bowl and toss with the vinegar and sugar. Refrigerate for 30 minutes.

For the sabayon, fill a pot with about 2 inches of water, place over medium heat, and bring to a gentle boil. Whisk the egg yolks, sugar, Marsala, and lemon zest in a stainless-steel or glass bowl until the mixture becomes frothy. Place the bowl over the pot and whisk vigorously for 4–5 minutes or until the sauce has thickened. Remove from the heat.

Working quickly, assemble the sandwiches. Spoon a generous amount of nectarines and apricots onto the bottom half of each bun, drizzle with a healthy amount of sabayon, and sprinkle with chopped pistachios. Sandwich closed with the top halves of the buns, and enjoy!

essential sauces

A sauce is that thing that brings everything together in a sandwich, helping it to shine the way it was meant to. Without sauce, we're looking at burgers without spicy mayo, steak sandwiches without earthy, punchy pestos, or even a breakfast sandwich without its spicy honey butter. As you've probably already guessed by now, I love sauces, and this chapter is full of the ones I turn to time and again.

What follows are what I call my "essential" sauces. These are the ones I think are worthy of their own little corner of this cookbook. The sauces that can stand their own and take on other dishes, such as salads, roasted vegetables, or any side dish that might be screaming for a little extra love. Make these sauces with their intended sandwich partners but come back and try them again for another use to switch things up a bit. I've included the name of the sandwich that I pair each sauce with in this book next to its title, and you can read a little more about each one there.

Lemon Garlic Aioli

(The Pretty One, page 112)

2 large egg yolks, at room temperature

3 cloves garlic, finely grated

1½ tsp Dijon mustard

Juice of ½ lemon

½ cup extra-virgin olive oil

½ tsp kosher salt

MAKES 1 CUP

Place the egg yolks, garlic, Dijon, lemon juice, and olive oil in a large mason jar or the container of your immersion blender. To make the aioli, you need to emulsify it. Emulsifying is taking two liquids that do not usually mix—in this case, the oil and the egg yolks (yolks are 50% water)—and turning them into a semi-stable mixture such as aioli or mayonnaise. Use your immersion blender to blend, moving it up and down until the aioli has thickened. Season with salt. This aioli can be stored in an airtight container in the fridge for up to a week.

Maple Mayo

Lemon Tarragon Brown Butter Mayo

(Another Sandwich for Dad, page 105)

¾ cup unsalted butter, cubed

1 large egg yolk

1 tsp Dijon mustard

Juice of ½ lemon

½ tsp kosher salt

1 tbsp roughly chopped fresh tarragon

MAKES 1 CUP

Melt the butter in a medium sauté pan over medium heat. Swirl the pan frequently to prevent it from burning. Cook until the butter browns and smells nutty, about 5–7 minutes. Remove the pan from the heat and immediately transfer the butter to a small mixing bowl to let cool completely.

Place the egg yolk, Dijon, lemon juice, and ¼ tsp salt in a blender. Blend on high for a minute and then slowly drizzle in the cooled brown butter as you continue to blend; you'll want to do this very slowly to ensure a lovely creamy consistency.

When ready, transfer the mayo to a bowl and gently fold in the tarragon. Taste and adjust the seasoning as needed. This mayo can be stored in an airtight container in the fridge for up to a week.

Maple Mayo

(A Breakfast Burger, page 60)

½ cup mayonnaise

1 tbsp maple syrup

1 tbsp grainy mustard

1 tsp hot sauce

MAKES A GENEROUS ½ CUP

Place all the ingredients in a mixing bowl and whisk to combine. This mayo can be stored in an airtight container in the fridge for up to a week.

Slow-Roasted Tomato Mayo

(Breakfast Frittata Sandwich, page 81)

2 cups cherry tomatoes, halved

2 tbsp extra-virgin olive oil

1 tsp kosher salt

1 tsp cracked black pepper

½ cup mayonnaise

MAKES 1 CUP

Preheat the oven to 400°F and line a baking sheet with foil. In a bowl, toss the tomatoes with the olive oil and season with salt and pepper. Place the tomatoes on the prepared baking sheet and roast for about 40 minutes, or until beautifully blistered and just slightly charred.

Remove from the oven and let cool. Once cooled, place the roasted tomatoes and all the juices pooled on the baking sheet in a food processor and blend until smooth (you can also use a high-speed blender if you prefer). Transfer the processed tomatoes to a bowl, add the mayo, and mix until nicely combined. This mayo will keep beautifully in an airtight container in the fridge for up to a week.

Turmeric Tahini Mayo

(Morgain's Saucebox, page 110)

½ cup mayonnaise

¼ cup tahini

1 tbsp maple syrup

Juice of ½ lemon

1 clove garlic, finely grated

½ tsp ground turmeric

½ tsp curry powder

¼ tsp kosher salt

MAKES ¾ CUP

Combine everything in a mixing bowl and whisk until smooth. As this mayo is quite thick, feel free to loosen it a bit with a few teaspoons of water if you like your sauce a bit thinner. You can store this mayo in an airtight container in the fridge for up to a week.

(Not So) Secret Sauce

(The Cover Model, page 95)

½ cup mayonnaise

1 tbsp ketchup

1 tbsp grainy mustard

1 tbsp yellow mustard

1 tsp vinegar-based hot sauce (more for a spicier sauce)

1 tsp runny honey

1 dill pickle, finely minced

½ tsp chili flakes

½ tsp cracked black pepper

MAKES ABOUT ⅔ CUP

In a mixing bowl, stir together all the ingredients until nicely combined. The sauce can be stored in an airtight container in the fridge for a week.

Slow-Roasted Tomato Mayo

Lemon Tartar Sauce

Lemon Tartar Sauce

(The Fish Burger, page 172)

¼ cup mayonnaise

¼ cup Greek yogurt

1 shallot, finely minced

1 clove garlic, finely grated

1 dill pickle, finely minced

1 tbsp capers, chopped

1 tbsp chopped fresh dill

1 tsp grainy mustard

Zest of ½ lemon

½ tsp cracked black pepper

MAKES ABOUT ⅔ CUP

In a bowl, whisk together all the ingredients, then cover and refrigerate until needed. The sauce can be stored in an airtight container in the fridge for up to a week.

Russian Dressing

(The Pretty Happy Drew, page 114)

½ cup mayonnaise

2 tbsp ketchup

1 large dill pickle, finely minced

1 tsp Worcestershire sauce

1 tsp hot sauce

1½ tsp creamed horseradish

Zest of 1 lemon

1 tsp sweet paprika

½ tsp dry mustard

MAKES ABOUT ⅔ CUP

Place everything in a mixing bowl and mix until fully incorporated. The dressing can be stored in an airtight container in the fridge for a week.

Avocado Spread

(The BLFGT, page 33)

2 avocados, peeled and pitted

¼ cup Greek yogurt

2 tbsp chopped fresh cilantro

Juice of 1 lime

1 tsp kosher salt

½ tsp cracked black pepper

MAKES ABOUT 2 CUPS

This spread can be made either smooth or chunky. Place all the ingredients in a mini or regular food processor and blitz until smooth. If you prefer something chunkier, place all the ingredients in a bowl and mash with a fork until you reach the desired consistency. This spread can be stored in an airtight container for a few days, but it's best used right away.

Spiced Peanut Sauce

(Stop Hating Eggplant, page 89)

½ cup crunchy or smooth natural peanut butter (only use natural; i.e., no sugar added) or try the recipe on page 50

½-inch knob fresh ginger, finely grated

2 cloves garlic, finely grated

1 tbsp rice wine vinegar

1 tbsp runny honey

1 tbsp soy sauce

1 tbsp chili crisp (if you can't find chili crisp, use 1 tsp chili flakes)

6–7 tbsp warm water (depending on how thin you like your sauce)

MAKES ABOUT 1 CUP

In a mixing bowl, whisk to combine all the ingredients except the water. Slowly add a bit of water and continue to whisk until your desired consistency is reached. Add more water if you like your sauce to be a bit runnier. This sauce can be stored in an airtight container in the fridge for up to a week.

Spicy Honey Butter

(The Originator, page 64)

⅓ cup unsalted butter

½ tsp sweet paprika

½ tsp cayenne

2 tbsp runny honey

Pinch of kosher salt and cracked black pepper

MAKES ABOUT ½ CUP

Combine the butter, paprika, cayenne, honey, salt, and pepper in a small pot over medium-high heat. Let the butter melt and whisk until beautifully combined.

Avocado Spread

Citrus BBQ Sauce

(The Pretty One, page 112)

1½ cups ketchup

Zest and juice of 1 lime

Zest and juice of 1 orange

¼ cup dark molasses

3 tbsp apple cider vinegar

1 tbsp sriracha (optional)

1 tbsp Worcestershire sauce

1 tbsp Dijon mustard

1 tsp smoked paprika

1 tsp onion powder

1 tsp kosher salt

½ tsp garlic powder

¼ tsp liquid smoke (optional)

MAKES 2½ CUPS

In a medium pot over medium heat, combine the ketchup, lime and orange juices (not the zest quite yet!), molasses, vinegar, sriracha (if using), Worcestershire, Dijon, smoked paprika, onion powder, salt, garlic powder, and liquid smoke (if using). Mix well and bring to a boil. Reduce the heat to low and let the sauce simmer for about 20–25 minutes or until thickened. Remove from the heat and stir in the lime and orange zest. Allow to cool completely before transferring to a mason jar. This sauce will keep in the fridge for up to 3 weeks.

Grainy Mustard

(A Cuban Sandwich, page 181)

⅓ cup yellow mustard seeds

⅓ cup brown mustard seeds

½ cup apple cider vinegar

½ cup water

2 tbsp brown sugar

1 tsp kosher salt

MAKES 1½ CUPS

Place all the ingredients in a jar, close tightly, and shake until well combined. Place on the counter overnight to allow the mustard seeds to soak. Once soaked, pour the contents of the jar into a blender and blend for a few minutes. This mustard can be stored in an airtight container in the fridge for up to 2 months.

Blue Cheese Sauce

(Sausage on a Bun: 3 Ways, page 38)

¼ cup sour cream

¼ cup mayonnaise

⅓ cup crumbled blue cheese

1–2 tbsp heavy cream (depending on how thick you want the sauce)

1 tsp cracked black pepper

MAKES ABOUT 1 CUP

Place everything in a bowl and mix until fully incorporated. Feel free to break up the blue cheese into small pieces or keep some larger chunks for a bit more texture. This sauce can be stored in an airtight container in the fridge for up to a week.

Roasted Garlic Sauce

(A Garlic Chicken Sandwich, page 183)

2 heads garlic

1 tbsp extra-virgin olive oil

1 tsp kosher salt

1 tsp cracked black pepper

2 tbsp unsalted butter

2 tbsp all-purpose flour

1 cup whole milk

½ cup finely grated Asiago

MAKES 1½ CUPS

Preheat the oven to 350°F. Cut the tops off the garlic bulbs and discard. Place the bulbs on a piece of foil. Coat the garlic with olive oil and season with ½ tsp salt and ½ tsp pepper. Wrap tightly into a package and place on a baking sheet. Roast in the oven for 40 minutes. Carefully unwrap the garlic and set aside to cool. Once cool, squeeze out the roasted garlic cloves into a small bowl. Mash until smooth, taking in the sweet and slightly caramel scent that's sure to be filling your kitchen.

This sauce can be stored in an airtight container in the fridge for up to 3 days. Gently reheat in a saucepan on low heat to bring it back to life, adding a splash or two of milk until your desired consistency is reached.

Fresh Herb Béchamel

(Croque Madame, page 67)

4 tbsp unsalted butter

1 large or 2 small shallots, finely minced

2 cloves garlic, finely grated

4 tbsp all-purpose flour

2 cups buttermilk

½ tsp lemon juice

⅓ cup finely chopped fresh dill and chives

1½ tsp Dijon mustard

1 tsp kosher salt

½ tsp cracked black pepper

MAKES 2 CUPS

Melt the butter in a medium pot over medium heat. Add the shallots and garlic and sauté for 1 minute. Add the flour and whisk until thoroughly combined and a roux has formed. (What is a roux? It's a mixture of equal parts flour and fat—in this case, butter—combined and cooked and used as a thickening agent.) Slowly pour in the buttermilk and whisk constantly until the sauce has smoothed and thickened, about 3–4 minutes. Remove from the heat and stir in the lemon juice, herbs, Dijon, and salt and pepper.

This sauce will store nicely in the fridge for up to 3 days. Gently reheat in a saucepan on low heat, adding a few splashes of milk until loosened.

Collard Green Pesto

(The Meatball, page 203)

3 cups roughly chopped collard greens (stems removed)

1 cup roughly chopped purple kale (stems removed)

⅓ cup macadamia nuts

2 cloves garlic

1 cup finely grated parmesan

Zest and juice of 1 lemon

½ tsp chili flakes

1 tsp kosher salt

⅓ cup extra-virgin olive oil

MAKES ABOUT 1½ CUPS

Place the collard greens, kale, macadamia nuts, garlic, parmesan, lemon zest and juice, chili flakes, and salt in a food processor. Blitz for a few seconds to get things moving, then, with the motor running, slowly drizzle in the oil and continue to process until smooth. This pesto can be stored in an airtight container in the fridge for up to a week.

Collard Green Pesto

Red Onion & Bacon Jam

(A Very Loud Burger, page 160)

1 (12 oz/340 g) package bacon, chopped into small pieces

3 medium red onions, thinly sliced

2 cloves garlic, finely minced

1½ tsp dried oregano

½ cup dark brown sugar

½ cup apple cider vinegar

2 tbsp Dijon mustard

1 tbsp grainy mustard

½ tsp chili flakes

MAKES 3 CUPS

Heat a large sauté pan over medium-high heat and add the chopped bacon (don't let your bacon come to room temperature before you cut it; cut it directly from the fridge and you'll have a much easier time slicing). Cook, stirring every so often, until it crisps up, about 10–12 minutes. Remove the bacon to a bowl and transfer about half of the fat from the pan to a mug or bowl (see page 163).

Reduce the heat to medium, add the onions to the pan, and sauté, occasionally stirring, until they have nicely softened, about 10 minutes. If you notice the bottom of the pan starting to burn slightly, add a splash of water and scrape down the pan with a wooden spoon. Add the garlic and oregano and continue to sauté for another few minutes. Add the brown sugar, vinegar, mustards, and chili flakes and bring the mixture to a boil. Reduce the heat to low, add the reserved bacon, and simmer for 35–40 minutes, stirring occasionally. At this point, the jam will have thickened nicely and can be set aside and cooled. Once cool, it will keep in an airtight container in your fridge for up to 2 weeks.

The Sandwich Questionnaire

1.

What is your idea of the perfect sandwich?

2.

What is your idea of the worst sandwich?

3.

If you were a sandwich, which sandwich would you be?

4.

What is the best filling a sandwich can have?

5.

What is the worst filling a sandwich can have?

6.

What is your favorite type of bread when making a sandwich?

7.

What is your least favorite type of bread when making a sandwich?

8.

Which five people, living or dead, would you want at your next sandwich party, and why?

9.

If a sandwich were to be named after you, what would it be called?

10.

What is the most overrated sandwich?

11.

What is the most underrated sandwich?

12.

In five words, describe a sandwich.

13.

Where and when did you eat your favorite sandwich?

14.

What is your favorite sandwich memory?

15.

Which type of sandwich have you eaten the most in your life?

16.

What was the last sandwich you ate?

17.

What was the first sandwich you ever ate?

18.

Is an open-faced sandwich really a sandwich?

19.

If you could only eat one sandwich again for the rest of your life, what would it be?

20.

Who makes the best sandwiches?

Thank You, Sandwich Lovers

I have been asked the question many times: "When are *you* going to write a cookbook?" Being a food stylist and working in television doing cooking segments, I get why people might be curious, but I never really knew how to answer. Not because I didn't want to write one, but because I really didn't know what a cookbook with my name on it would even begin to look like. During the pandemic I had a lot of time to think and dream about that cookbook (and dream and think and think and dream!). It was on a flight home from the UK that I had that "aha!" moment—at least I think that's what it was. All at once, like a dam breached by inspiration, everything came flooding into my brain while I sat, semi-frozen, gazing out the window and into the clouds. "A sandwich cookbook!?" I said to myself. Everyone loves sandwiches, right? What could be better? Writing this book has been an enormously fulfilling process. From the onset, when my proposal was accepted, to developing and testing the recipes, to feeding them to my cherished circle of friends and family, I could not have done it alone.

Mom, Dad, and Carm, I can't thank you enough for everything you've taught me. I love you beyond words and wish you'd been able to see this book come to life.

To my twin brother, Ryan. Your steadfast devotion to this book and your unwavering support mean so much. You're the best big little brother a guy could ask for! Greg, Paul, Angie, and Afsah, thank you for your years of encouragement.

The images, which are tremendously important to me, were a labor of love, and I was lucky enough to have an extremely skilled partner in my photographer, all-around first-class human Sébastien Dubois-Didcock. Thank you for enduring the months and months of phone calls, emails, WhatsApp messages, and sometimes, I'm sure, doltish questions I threw your way. Your enormous talent and technique brought this book to life, and it would not be what it is without you. *Merci beacoup*, Sébastien!

An enormous thank-you to my gifted illustrator, Joel Malkin, whose thoughtful and exquisite illustrations grace these pages. Your invaluable contribution has given this book an extra dose of magic.

A massive thank-you and tons of sandwich love to my editor extraordinaire, Lindsay Paterson (who endured endless rewrites on my part—thank you for your patience!). Your constant enthusiasm for this book and your trust in me mean the world. Katherine Stopa, thank you for jumping on the sandwich train before the last stop! Your zest for these sandwiches is extremely appreciated. To Michelle Arbus, thank you for taking that call; it changed everything! To my publisher, Robert McCullough, thank you for seeing my vision and for allowing me to unleash this book into the universe. To Jen Griffiths, you've designed the book of my dreams and I can't thank you enough. To Carly Watters, thank you for taking me on and for your guidance on this journey.

Thank you to my mighty Toronto crew. My dear Gillian Taylor, your beautiful work graces many of the pages of this book and it would not be what it is without you, I'm beyond grateful. Janette Mitchell; you're a force, woman! Testing recipes, food styling, hand modeling, shopping, and doling out bird facts to distract me on set—thank you! Amber Joliat, I'm blown away by your resilience. Thank you for always reminding me to breathe (and I certainly needed that on more days than not). To Keelan Smith, for the years and years (and years!) of support (and the many, many gin and tonics), and for always swooping in when I needed you the most—it is always appreciated, my dear friend. To Sonia Schuster: while we may have met in the gym, we truly bonded over our shared love of all things sweet. You'll always be my cookie queen. Eimear De La Rosa-Brazil, thank you for always laughing at my jokes, and for knowing what I needed, even if I didn't. To my friend Zeke and my sister-law Afsah, thank you for lending me your most perfect sandwich-holding hands. Lily Hu, thank you for the hustle on set. You are a rock star! An enormous amount of gratitude to Catherine Dubois, who graciously let me invade her home for two weeks to shoot the majority of this cookbook; you're a gem! RIP to all that bread!

To the Toronto tasters: Gavin, Jenn, and Keelan, thank you so much for hosting. Chelsie, Mike, Amber, Nik, Janette, Andy, Geoff, Cat, Ashton, Michelle, Dave, June Anne, Shane, and Karen, thank you for tasting endless amounts of sandwiches—your feedback helped shape this book.

To my phenomenal UK crew: Morgain Fitzpatrick and Gary Bailey, there are no words. Your love of sandwiches, in particular drunken late-night sandwiches and late-morning hungover sandwiches, is the reason this book was born. Thank you for the years of guidance, friendship, laughter, and trivia. Here's to more drag shows, weekend getaways, and lost credit cards. My forever partners in crime.

To the UK tasters: Jo, Lucy, Beth, Dave, Andy, Chris, and Rob, your enthusiasm for those sandwiches was simply delicious.

To my outstanding Paris crew: Sébastien, Léa, and Olive, a huge thank-you for allowing me to shoot part of this book in your house; I'll always be grateful. And to Alex, Nesreen, and Khady for being so generous with your time.

To my Plutino family, especially Roseanna and Jenna, thank you for everything you've brought my way over the years, much love.

To Krista Look and Portia Corman, much gratitude to you both for the years of mentorship I received, and for being such big supporters of mine from the start. I can't begin to tell you how much that has meant to me.

And finally, to my *Your Morning* family at CTV. First and foremost, Sush Rao, thank you for bringing me on board, pushing me to take the big leap in front of the camera, and always being such a supportive friend. Marisa Zucaro, Jen MacLean, Jennifer Sue, Shannon Chambers, Paul Hughes, Katie Jamieson, Carolyn Rossetto, Attila Baraczka, Trish Bradley, Kamal Bandukwala, Devon Johnson, Heather Milne, Tara Stanton, Natasha Dhanipersad, Brad MacDonald, Chris Corrado, Dave Harnden, Steve McCann, Jessica Nevin, Alvin Kwan, Claire Hall, Aditi Kodesia, Breanna Xavier-Carter, Nikolas Rajic, Kelly Medeiros, Amanda Oosterman, Emily Bevan, George Kalogiros, and Oneil Mangal, I'm blown away by your kindness and encouragement. And to the hosts who have been the very best live TV teachers a guy could ask for, Lindsey Deluce, Anne-Marie Mediwake, Kelsey McEwen, and Ben Mulroney, thank you from the bottom of my sandwich-loving heart for making me look good and always having my back.

I love every single sandwich in this book, and I'm eager for you to find your favorite. Happy sandwich making, my friends.

Index

The Pretty Happy Drew (page 114)